WRITERS AND CRITICS

Chief Editor

A. NORMAN JEFFARES

Advisory Editors

DAVID DAICHES

C. P. SNOW

ROBERT FROST is a paradox: a traditional poet who made formal bounds for his poetry, but never limited its subject-matter; and a nature poet whose philosophy went far beyond the usual experiences of the country-man. This detailed study of Frost's poetry, from the early poems written before the First World War to those which he published in the last year of his long and fruitful life, gives due emphasis to Frost as a man and writer who was keenly aware of the place and importance of both intellect and emotion in poetry.

Miss Jennings, who is herself a poet, not only gives her own views on Frost, but also analyses and evaluates the opinions of those critics who have, with a few exceptions, tended to miss the deeper resonances and significance of a poet who often seems so simple, but is in fact quite as complex in his message and meaning as any of the great poetical innovators of our time.

FROST

ELIZABETH JENNINGS

OLIVER AND BOYD
EDINBURGH AND LONDON

OLIVER AND BOYD LTD
Tweeddale Court
Edinburgh 1

39A Welbeck Street
London, W. 1

First published 1964

Printed in Great Britain for Oliver and Boyd Ltd
by Robert MacLehose and Co. Ltd, Glasgow

CONTENTS

ACKNOWLEDGMENTS

For permission to quote from Robert Frost's works acknowledgments are due to Jonathan Cape Ltd.

Acknowledgments are also due to the following: Miss Babette Deutsch and Doubleday & Co. (Babette Deutsch: *Poetry in Our Time*); Alfred A. Knopf, Inc. (Randall Jarrell: *Poetry and the Age*); Henry Regnery Company (Louise Bogan: *Achievement in American Poetry*); Charles Scribner & Sons (A. Alvarez: *The Shaping Spirit*); University of Minnesota Press (Lawrance Thompson: *Robert Frost*).

The photograph on the front cover is reproduced by permission of the Associated Press Ltd.

E.J.

CHAPTER I

INTRODUCTION

Of all the well-established and much venerated American poets, Robert Frost is probably the most popular and the least criticised. His work appears regularly in school anthologies, yet he himself has failed to receive the close critical attention which has, for example, been accorded so freely to Wallace Stevens. Frost has been widely honoured in England and in the United States, and his poems have never been subject to the fluctuations of literary taste and fashions. Yet he himself has seldom received that careful critical analysis, that exacting ex-egesis which is such a popular literary activity nowadays. The main reason for this is, of course, that Frost has never belonged to any literary movements; he never took part in the great modernist battles, in the search for new forms and new language. He escaped both the assistance and the dangers of literary alignments. Thus, during his stay in England before and in the early part of the First World War, he never became so attached to the "Georgian" poetic idiom that he could be truly called a member of that movement. Frost has never been in or out of fashion, but always respected, even if sometimes taken too much for granted.

Though Frost knew Pound who read and approved of his early work, he was never a modernist writer. Yet it should not be assumed that his work was, or is, wholly traditional. He is one of those poets who not only forge their own idiom and versification but who also create the context in which that work will appear at its best and most acceptable. Frost's gnomic simplicity and rustic clarity, in fact, often conceal remarkable subtleties and some extremely disturbing elements. The accommodating quality of his poems, is often only a surface matter. Frost, indeed, is primarily a philosophical poet and also a highly skilled practitioner of all the arts and artifices of verse.

Frost does not easily lay himself open to the explicator or the searcher for similarities. He is, in fact, in some ways a very fugitive poet. He distrusts large words and grandiose claims. As we can see from some of his own almost off-hand comments on his work (in an interview given to *The Paris Review*),[1] he is not too eager to discuss his poetry. Thus he refuses either to be loftily mysterious or to give complex psychological motives for the making of his poems; he declares that "every thought, poetical or otherwise, every thought is a feat of association," that "the whole thing is performance and prowess and feats of association," and that "when they want to know about inspiration, I tell them it's mostly animus."

Even if we make allowances for the bravado which this kind of interview induces in a man of Frost's wit and reticence, we must still take seriously the declarations he makes about his own attitude to his work. Moreover, he makes some remarks of extraordinary interest, as, for instance, in the comments on his fascination with science, and with astronomy in particular. Frost also reveals himself quite fearlessly in this interview when he says:

See, I haven't led a literary life. These fellows, they *really* work away with their prose trying to describe themselves and understand themselves, and so on. I don't do that. I don't want to know too much about myself. . . . These fellows are all literary men. I don't have hours; I don't work at it, you know. I'm not a farmer, that's no pose of mine. But I have farmed some, and I putter around. And I walk and I live with other people. Like to talk a lot.

Such disclaimers as these may, of course, be Frost's way of protecting himself from the prying scrutinies of critics and journalists; when this is said, however, one is left with the impression of a man who has too much reverence for his own talent to want to risk damaging it either by self-questioning or by trying to analyse it too much. Frost does all the questioning he needs to do *within* his poems; and it may be that he is suspicious of probing inquiries about his work simply because he distrusts their effect on poems which may be working in his mind but which are not as yet written. Most poets have, surely, experienced this suspicion of prose inquiries which can so often mean death to a growing poem.

What is also illuminating in Frost's interview with *The Paris Review* is the clear evidence he gives us that he is by no means the rustic homespun poet-cum-farmer that some commentators on his work have implied. He is, above all, a whole-hearted writer, a man who has assigned to poetry many of the things which other men enshrine in a personal religion or philosophy.

Frost has no place in the great poetic experiments of this century; his development has been entirely his own. If his style has changed, if his thought has become increasingly complex over the years—that is entirely Frost's affair. Truthfully, though often indirectly, his poems chart his own inner world; and, oddly enough, this poet who appears to be gazing constantly at the natural world, is also very much an *inward* poet. He does not rearrange nature, as Wallace Stevens did, or view it allegorically, as Edwin Muir did. He never, in fact, imposes himself on the external world. Instead, he strikes an extremely delicate balance in his poems between the world he sees and works in and the processes of thought and emotion which he is always keenly aware of in himself. When this balance fails, Frost's poems become either merely didactic, on the one hand, or else descriptive, on the other: but when they succeed, they com-

municate an almost visionary quality—a vision which is
immanent, not transcendent.

If Frost has formed a solitary movement of his own, a
strong but isolated element in modern American poetry
—if, as A. Alvarez[2] has asserted, it is hard "to recognise
how much of the tradition he merely took over and how
much he had to make up for himself"—this fact alone has
been responsible for a certain neglect of his work on the
part of the more advanced literary critics. It is, however,
a shallow judgment which dismisses Frost as merely a
dexterous purveyor of homely wisdom. Alvarez has himself gone to some lengths to explain Frost's method and
popularity with the general public, but he has not
succeeded in localising it. For the fact is that Frost's
work tends to resist clever definitions and easy interpre-
tations; thus, Alvarez only displays his own lack of
understanding when he declares, ". . . he [Frost] is not a
nature poet; his work has none of that personal interpretative weight. He is a country poet, whose business is
to live with nature rather than through it." If the latter
part of this passage is slightly obscure, the former bears
witness to a common misunderstanding of Frost's work.
For an unprejudiced reading of his poems will, I am sure,
reveal just that "personal interpretative weight" which
Alvarez denies to it.

Because Frost has never been associated with Pound,
Eliot, or any of the great twentieth-century poetic
innovators, it would be wrong to conclude that his poems
are written in a sort of "timeless" language, an idiom
belonging to no particular age or country. Indeed, one of
the most striking things about his work is its relevance to
our own time; only in its earliest manifestations does it
give one the sense of being slightly archaic or even dated.
One of the reasons for this is Frost's conversational,
almost casual manner. Many of his poems sound like the
poet either ruminating or else talking to his friends; such
poems as these are written in "the language of ordinary

men," though other, more complex ones, whose pattern of thought is closely bound into their poetic texture, are by no means always simple or straightforward.

The gnomic or aphoristic element is, perhaps, the one most familiar to the casual reader of Frost. Those of his poems which are most frequently anthologised tend to belong to this *genre*. Thus many people who would scarcely recognise much of Frost's later work are perfectly familiar with, for example, these lines from "Reluctance":

> Ah, when to the heart of man
>   Was it ever less than a treason
> To go with the drift of things,
>   To yield with a grace to reason,
> And bow and accept the end
>   Of a love or a season?

with this, from "Mending Wall":

> Something there is that doesn't love a wall. . . .

with these, from "The Road Not Taken":

> I shall be telling this with a sigh
> Somewhere ages and ages hence:
> Two roads diverged in a wood, and I—
> I took the one less traveled by,
> And that has made all the difference.

and these, from "Stopping by Woods on a Snowy Evening":

> The woods are lovely, dark and deep,
> But I have promises to keep,
> And miles to go before I sleep,
> And miles to go before I sleep.

These lines may well be responsible for giving many people the idea that Frost is primarily a moralising poet, that his poems are, above all other considerations, didactic in intent. Yet anyone who reads his poems with care and sympathy will realise how hard Frost works for his conclusions, how aptly and beautifully they arise out of their pure lyric contexts, how deftly and justly they conclude a reflective or descriptive poem; one feels, in fact, that Frost's conclusions or "directives" are quite as organic as the other elements of his poems. He has said himself, in a discussion on rhyme, "I want to be unable to tell which of those he thought of first. If there's any trick about it, putting the better one first so as to deceive me, I can tell pretty soon." Frost has a very deep distrust of anything that seems like trickery in poetry; he would abhor the remark I once heard a young American poet making about his own poetry—"You can fake it, but you got to fake it good." Truth to experience is the ultimate criterion with Frost and throughout his life he has remained faithful to his own dictum that "Poetry begins in delight and ends in wisdom."

Robert Frost was born in San Francisco (a fact which may seem surprising, since, for most of his life, he has been regarded as a deeply-rooted New England poet) in 1874. His father was a New Englander, but his mother was an emigrant from Scotland. The child was named after the famous Southern general, Robert E. Lee. Frost remained in San Francisco until he was eleven, when his father died of tuberculosis. He and his mother and younger sister then settled in Salem, New Hampshire, where his mother taught in the school which her children attended.

Frost refused to read any book by himself until he was twelve years old, and it was at the Lawrence High School that he discovered a taste for study and learning. He graduated as class poet in 1892 and then for a short time attended Dartmouth College. During the next few years, like so many young American poets today, he tried various jobs including teaching, newspaper reporting, and mill work. Always, however, his leisure time was occupied in writing poetry. In 1895 he married and, for two years after that, helped his mother manage a small private school in Lawrence. He then went to Harvard for two years, with the intention of training himself to be a college teacher. However, it soon became plain to him that the academic world did not suit his temperament; from the world of learning he turned to poultry farming.

All this time, Frost was suffering from various illnesses, probably nervous in origin. After a year of teaching psychology, he decided to gamble everything on his poetry. With this end in view, he took his wife and four children to England, and there rented a house in Beaconsfield.

Frost's first book, *A Boy's Will*, was accepted by the first English publisher to whom he sent it and appeared in 1913. His dramatic dialogues and other poems, published in book form under the title *North of Boston*, were published in 1914 and well received by discriminating readers in Britain. Thus when Frost returned with his family to the United States early in 1914, he had already made something of a reputation for himself. More important for his future development, he had come under the influence of Edward Thomas, who died during the First World War. In a later poem, called "To E.T.," Frost indicates something of what Thomas's friendship meant to him:

> You went to meet the shell's embrace of fire
> On Vimy ridge, and when you fell that day
> The war seemed over more for you than me,
> But now for me than you—the other way.
>
> How over, though, for even me who knew
> The foe thrust back unsafe beyond the Rhine,
> If I was not to speak of it to you
> And see you pleased once more with words of mine?

Frost published his first book of poems comparatively late: but this means that his earliest printed work has his unique tone of voice, that ring of slightly ironic authority which was later to become so characteristic of his poetry. He found his voice with his first book of poems; he has seldom needed to change it, only to widen its range and deepen its cadences.

When Frost returned to the United States, he bought a small farm in New Hampshire and it is probably this fact, together with his extreme shyness, which has resulted in his being regarded as the lonely farmer-poet, the communer with nature, the observer of wild things. The truth is, however, that he by no means led a sheltered life; he needed money badly and was soon giving public lectures and readings. Also, in spite of his reiterated dislike of academic affairs, he was one of the first American poets to seek jobs as poet-in-residence on the campus of various universities. Frost is at first sight, therefore, rather an anomaly—a farmer who professed to despise the academic life, profiting from the freedom and intellectual excitement which such a life can offer; a poet who apparently longed for solitude willingly entering the market-place. When we examine Frost's early poetic career more closely, we soon discover that the apparent concessions he made were only made in order that he might have more time and stimulus to write. The interchange of ideas which he found in the universities suited his inquiring mind (we must not forget his deep interest in psychology and astronomy), while the presence of young people studying, trying to write, and manifesting a lively concern with the making of poems in itself was stimulating for Frost; it is seldom, after all, that literary stimulation works only one way between teacher and pupil.

But perhaps more important than anything else is the fact that by the early nineteen-twenties, Frost had consolidated his ideas to some extent. He was not open to influence and fashion in the way a younger man might have been. He had found his own voice and he had also begun to touch on many of the subjects which were to absorb him so deeply in his later work. It is important to remember that Frost was from the beginning a philosophical poet; he did not start by writing simple and charming rustic poems which relied for their effect on the exploitation of the picturesque. The accuracy of his observation is certainly apparent in his earliest work, but what is even more striking is the philosophical anxiety, the stoical sadness—qualities which we find displayed far more obviously and deliberately in later poems. Something of this later power is undoubtedly present, nevertheless, in the first poem in *A Boy's Will* entitled "Into my Own":

> One of my wishes is that those dark trees,
> So old and firm they scarcely show the breeze,
> Were not, as 'twere, the merest mask of gloom,
> But stretched away unto the edge of doom.
>
> I should not be withheld but that some day
> Into their vastness I should steal away. . . .

Frost was not at first popular with the general public; though well received by a number of critics and poetry-lovers, his earliest books were not widely acclaimed. Not until he was forty did he begin to receive both academic honours and that sort of public popularity which he has never lost. Few other English or American poets have been rewarded with such a cluster of academic honours both in the United States and in England (Frost was recently honoured both at Oxford and Cambridge). But it is not only the academic world which has shown itself so willing to accept and pay tribute to this poet. And, of course, as so often happens in the literary world, Frost's very popularity has laid him open to the adverse criticism of certain scholars and critics. Yvor Winters,[3] in an essay entitled "Robert Frost or the Spiritual Drifter as Poet," has said:

B

A popular poet is always a spectacle of some interest, for poetry in general is not popular; and when the popular poet is also within limits a distinguished poet, the spectacle is even more curious, for commonly it is bad poetry which is popular. When we encounter such a spectacle, we may be reasonably sure of finding certain social and historical reasons for the popularity.

Winters goes on to explain Frost's popularity on the grounds that he has been wrong-headedly regarded as a classical poet (though just why this should make for popularity is more obscure). Winters also gives a simpler and more acceptable reason, namely that

Frost writes of rural subjects and the American reader of our time has an affection for rural subjects which is partly the product of the Romantic sentimentalization of "nature", but which is partly also a nostalgic looking back to the rural life which predominated in this nation a generation or two ago.

Ivor Winters is, of course, well known for his provocative opinions, and Frost is not the only twentieth-century American poet who has been attacked by him; Wallace Stevens and Hart Crane have also received their share of adverse criticism. Winters starts from a theory of reason (he is a Thomist without the theological framework) and castigates anything which appears to be not immediately amenable to reason; he states unequivocally that "The poet . . . must make a rational statement about an experience, and as rationality is a part of the medium, the ultimate value of the poem will depend in a fair measure on the soundness of the rationality." Few other critics, perhaps, would take such a firm stand on rationality; it would seem to them that intuition and imagination are more properly the source of poetry. To say this is not to deny reason but simply to say that reason is not poetry's only or main support.

Before we examine the poems in detail, and thus demonstrate how wrong-headed Winters' strictures really are, it is sufficient to quote another more enthusiastic critic of Frost, Randall Jarrell;[4] "To feel this fear of God and to go ahead in spite of it, Frost says, is man's principal virtue, courage. . ." and again, "He has a thorough scepticism about that tame revenge, justice, and a cold certainty that nothing but mercy will do for *us*. What he really warms to is a rejection beyond either justice or mercy."

To play one critic off against another does not, of course, prove anything. One thing it can do, however, and that is to show us that Frost's poems are not moral treatises, that they are to be responded to rather than to be argued about. It is ironic that Winters, though he has little use for Frost as a philosopher, does criticise his work as if it were a series of moral injunctions rather than a collection of poems.

It is true that many of Frost's poems carry a moral, but the moral is usually presented either as an argument running through a descriptive or sensuous lyric, or as part of a dramatic situation. It is very seldom indeed that Frost makes his "lessons" as overt and obvious as Wordsworth sometimes did. Both are poets who turn to nature for moral and emotional elevation or with a certain acquiescent desolation. But both men—and this fact is too often forgotten in critiques of their work—are poets of mood. They are, in the best sense, exploiters of moods, looters of the present moment, and, in their more complex states of mind, searchers after symbols. At times, Frost's symbols, analogies, and equivalences too readily assert themselves; the reader feels that they have not been sufficiently worked for, that they emerge too easily from the general shape and design of the poem. Cleanth Brooks[5] has said, "Frost's themes are frequently stated overtly, outside the symbolical method; the poet comes downstage to philosophize explicitly," but he goes on to add,

At his best, of course, Frost does not philosophize. The anecdote is absorbed into symbol. The method of indirection operates fully: the sense of realistic detail, the air of casual comment, are employed to build up and intensify a serious effect.

This last comment reminds us of a central truth about Frost which is too often overlooked; I mean the undoubted fact that he is, and always has been, an intensely dedicated and self-conscious artist. The way in which, in *The Paris Review* interview, he shies away from the too searching questions of his interviewers is itself an indication that Frost takes his work very seriously indeed. It is usually the unimportant writers who talk most volubly about their work. The literary tradition into which Frost's work broadly fits is a pastoral one, though he certainly does not have much affinity with the delicate world of shepherds and shepherdesses with which Spenser worked in *The Shepherd's Calendar*; as John F. Lynen[6] has said,

> If the pastoral tradition had long since lost its validity, how was he [Frost] to write a poetry essentially pastoral? The answer to this question becomes apparent when one recalls the distinction between pastoralism as a kind of poetic structure and pastoralism in the narrower sense of a particular tradition. It was the tradition that had withered; the fundamental form remained as a potential.

And as Lynen indicates elsewhere, the pastoral form, with its stress on two utterly contrasted ways of life, was peculiarly amenable to the sense of duality which is an essential, perhaps the central, part of Frost's poetic vision. In his poems, contraries are constantly being set side by side—human life and mechanical power, living nature and the insensate soil, light and darkness, good and evil, and so on. The pastoral mode is a form which adapts itself easily to analogy. It is looser, more adaptable to new treatment than traditional allegory; it does not demand the note of sententiousness or moralising which the allegorical method usually implies. At its best—as in, for example, "Stopping by Woods on a Snowy Evening" —Frost has created a new kind of symbolism out of the outmoded, conventional pastoralism. As Lynen says

> The indirect and subtly suggestive quality of its ["Stopping by Woods on a Snowy Evening"] symbolism results from his preference for implication rather than explicit statement. He does not interpret the scene; he uses it as the medium through which to view reality.

Robert Frost has been called many things—a symbolist, a spiritual drifter, a homespun philosopher, a lyricist, a moraliser, a preacher, a farmer who writes verse. It is perhaps the surface simplicity of his poetry which has enabled so many different critics to impose their own idea of what he is upon his work. Frost has suffered from this. Very little of his work is really simple, yet his poetry does undoubtedly yield something even to the most casual reading. What is this "something," this quality which is surely responsible for Frost's present enormous popularity? It is, in the first place, an honest, steady attitude to the reader, a willingness to admit that he or she will quickly understand and feel what Frost is presenting. This quality expresses itself in the *tone* of the poems, a tone which is more than a question of a similarity to ordinary conversation. A conversational note is not in itself a poetic virtue. Frost's tone—easy and off-hand as it so often sounds—is really full of artistry. The music is always decisive, yet seldom over-intrusive, the language, however simple, is always a matter of art rather than of ordinary life. These points are well illustrated in "Mowing," a poem which appeared in Frost's first book. Here, the rhymes echo but are never

too emphatic; the moraliser and the contemplative are in
perfect harmony:

There was never a sound beside the wood but one,
And that was my long scythe whispering on the
    ground.
What was it it whispered? I knew not well myself;
Perhaps it was something about the heat of the sun,
Something, perhaps, about the lack of sound—
And that was why it whispered and did not speak.

There is in Frost's early work a certain anthropomorphic
quality, a tendency to impute human attributes and
sensations to inanimate objects. This tendency becomes
much less marked in his later work, where the wish to
preach or point a moral is quite secondary to the visionary experience which Frost is trying to communicate.
"On Looking up by Chance at the Constellations" shows
how subtle and malleable Frost's method has become over
the years:

You'll wait a long, long time for anything much
To happen in heaven beyond the floats of cloud
And the Northern Lights that run like tingling nerves.
The sun and moon get crossed but they never touch,
Nor strike out fire from each other, nor crash out loud.

Perhaps the most obvious difference between this poem
and "Mowing" is in the poet's later eagerness to let
alone, to observe without wanting to alter, to meditate
without interfering. Briefly, Frost has become increasingly a contemplative poet, a man who watches before
he acts, who learns before he tries to teach. His contem-
plation is, however, involved with other human beings as
well as with nature. Indeed, the presence of other people
is often as much a necessity to Frost as that of *objets d'art*
was to Wallace Stevens. Frost's late poem, "All Revelation," expresses this fact very succinctly:

Eyes seeking the response of eyes
Bring out the stars, bring out the flowers,
Thus concentrating earth and skies
So none need be afraid of size.
All revelation has been ours.

"The Silken Tent," which appears in the same volume, shows how sure and delicate Frost has become in the handling of comparisons. The language and rhythm are beautifully poised here, and there is no sense of the poet straining for likenesses or metaphors. In this poem, the image and the idea, or the person, are perfectly united:

She is as in a field a silken tent
At midday when a sunny summer breeze
Has dried the dew and all its ropes relent,
So that in guys it gently sways at ease,
And its supporting central cedar pole,
That is its pinnacle to heavenward
And signifies the sureness of the soul,
Seems to owe naught to any single cord,
But strictly held by none, is loosely bound
By countless silken ties of love and thought
To everything on earth the compass round. . . .

In this poem the anthropomorphic element is almost imperceptible and where it does appear, as in "all its ropes relent," it seems entirely subservient to the main drift of the poem and, therefore, completely acceptable to the reader.

Robert Frost died early in 1963 at a great age. He started publishing his poems during the First World War and he went on writing and publishing through all the great literary movements and experiments in Britain and in the United States. While Pound and Eliot were forging a new language for poetry, while Wallace Stevens was making the study of perception and imagination the very subject-matter of his verse, Frost was steadily perfecting his own instrument. If his experiments with language and rhythm seem conservative and fugitive beside the more public innovations of Pound and Eliot, they were real experiments nonetheless. Frost's quiet struggles with words and music have undoubtedly had a purifying effect on the American poetic language. It is almost impossible to read a formal poem by a young American poet to-day without being aware of the presiding influence of Frost. His gentle irony, his absolute simplicity and honesty, his fastidious use of abstractions—these and many other qualities can be felt in the work of many of the younger poets, and it is from Frost that those qualities largely derive.

Frost is basically a philosophic poet who often uses the pastoral mode as a vehicle for his inquiries into the nature and meaning of life. His irony, didacticism and lyricism, all serve this end. Yet, so completely are form and content united in Frost's work, it is scarcely possible to remove the philosophical element in any given poem without completely dislocating it. Frost's early poems may seem easy to paraphrase (though this is often an illusion), but his late ones usually positively defy any attempt on the reader's part to reduce them to prose meanings. In the late poem, "Directive," the meaning, or message, is so intimately caught up into the verbal texture that it would be almost impossible even to imagine the content without the form. Frost's language is pure, direct, simple and conversational, yet what he has to say is extremely complex. The poem ends

> I have kept hidden in the instep arch
> Of an old cedar at the waterside
> A broken drinking goblet like the Grail
> Under a spell so the wrong ones can't find it,
> So can't get saved, as Saint Mark says they mustn't.
> (I stole the goblet from the children's playhouse.)
> Here are your waters and your watering-place.
> Drink and be whole again beyond confusion.

Frost's complexity is more the complexity of a riddle or a spell than that of a dry philosophical argument. His aphorisms have a quality of magic about them; the poet, one feels, is revealing a secret rather than simply teaching a lesson. This is made very clear in some short late poems, such as "A Mood Apart," which ends,

> But becoming aware of some boys from school
> Who had stopped outside the fence to spy,
> I stopped my song and almost heart,
> For any eye is an evil eye
> That looks in on to a mood apart.

The same quality is also apparent in "A Steeple on the House":

> What if it should turn out eternity
> Was but the steeple on our house of life
> That made our house of life a house of worship?
> We do not go up there to sleep at night.
> We do not go up there to live by day.
> Nor need we ever go up there to live.
> A spire and belfry coming on the roof
> Means that a soul is coming on the flesh.

Such a quietly explosive ending as this is more akin to magic than to metaphysics. For Frost, life is a mystery; poetry may penetrate a little way into that mystery but even it will never discover the whole truth. So Frost's poems are, as it were, partial revelations, notes on the way taken from one man's experience. Yet in spite of the intimately personal flavour of many of his poems, Frost is not an autobiographical or introspective writer. His first gaze is always outward and he turns inward to examine his own mind more to discover how the human mind functions than because he is specially interested in his own mental processes. He has, in fact, that splendid generalising power which we find in all major poets, but he starts always from a particular instance, a certain scene, a single man working, or a group of people.

In his interview with *The Paris Review*, Frost showed himself to be a poet who is not eager to examine the mechanism in himself which is responsible for the making of poems. He has—in spite of all the public honours and prizes which have been heaped upon him—always maintained his privacy and solitude.

Frost, then, is a poet who values solitude, a time to reflect and a time to be silent. He is the least public of poets yet, paradoxically, his direct manner, his calm tone, his simple language have made him the most popular and most loved of all modern American poets. This popularity is certainly based on an admiration for qualities which are really present in Frost's poems: but, nonetheless, his work is often misunderstood or admired for the wrong reasons. For Frost is a true visionary poet but a poet who has, as it were, brought his visions down to earth. His world is the world we all know and live in; his symbolism flowers naturally from the life and work of the New England countryside. His poems are neither allusive nor eclectic, yet his simplicity and directness are only superficial things. Beneath the easy movements of his verse, there is a mind at work which is as subtle as that of any poet of this century. To ignore the subtlety is to miss the true nature of Robert Frost's work, as well as to be unaware of a deeply orginal contemplative mind and a man of powerful feeling.

REFERENCES

1. *P.R.*, p. 89.
2. *S.S.*, p. 169.
3. *O.M.P.*, p. 191.
4. *P.A.*, p. 43.

5. *M.P.T.*, p. 116–17.
6. J. F. Lynen, *The Pastoral Art of Robert Frost*, New Haven 1960, p. 18.

CHAPTER II

A BOY'S WILL, NORTH OF BOSTON, MOUNTAIN INTERVAL, NEW HAMPSHIRE

If it is true that there have been no sudden developments in Frost's work, no abrupt switches of mood or new experiments, it is also true that his first book, *A Boy's Will*,[1] has more archaisms, more affinities with the English Georgian poets, than Frost's later work. The themes of the poems which the book contains—nostalgia, stoicism, a feeling of unity with the seasons and with country things—have remained constant. It is only the approach that has changed and become simpler and barer over the years. Yet even this early book contains poems which it would be hard to date if one came across them at random in an anthology, in particular "The Tuft of Flowers," "Mowing," and "Reluctance," the last poem in the book. Such poems as these already show the typically Frostian wedding of aphorism with description; the mingling is not perhaps complete yet, the "wisdom" sometimes seems awkwardly tagged onto the concrete scene, but the tendency is already there, if only in an embryonic form. And the sound of the poet's own voice is also already recognisable, even if it does not yet carry complete authority.

Nevertheless, some things in *A Boy's Will* do jar on us to-day. This book is undoubtedly dated, and dated in a way that Wallace Stevens's first book, for example, was not. Some of the worst faults of the poetry of the eighteen-nineties in England, as well as those of the Georgian poets, are certainly evident in *A Boy's Will*. One is halted by

both the archaicism and whimsy of such lines as the
following, from "My Butterfly":

> And I was glad for thee,
> And glad for me, I wist.

with these, from "October Mist":

> Retard the sun with gentle mist;
> Enchant the land with amethyst.

and these, from "Pan With Us":

> Pan came out of the woods one day,—
> His skin and his hair and his eyes were grey.

Lapses like these certainly make the reader uneasy, but at
least they have one distinct value: they throw into clear
relief the already developed virtues of Frost—the refusal
to indulge a small emotion, the determination to remain
calm in the most tragic circumstances. Here one might
cite the fine ending of "Reluctance," a stanza which
illustrates well Frost's gift for running thought easily
along a melodic line:

> Ah, when to the heart of man
>> Was it ever less than a treason
> To go with the drift of things,
>> To yield with a grace to reason,
> And bow and accept the end
>> Of a love or a season?

Frost's attitude towards religion is also less equivocal
in these early poems than it is in his later ones. There are
many invocations to God who, as a personal deity, is felt
as an immanent rather than as a transcendent being. In
"My Butterfly," Frost declares:

It seemed God let thee flutter from his gentle clasp.

and the same attitude is found in "The Trial by Existence":

> And very beautifully God limns,
> And tenderly, life's little dream.

and in "Revelation":

> But so with all, from babes that play
> At hide-and-seek to God afar,
> So all who hide too well away
> Must speak and tell us where they are.

This God may be "afar" but he is also, one feels, within reach, available to man and aware of all his doings. On the other hand, Frost's concept of evil, as it is manifested in his earliest poems, is sometimes childish to the point of fatuity. In "The Demiurge's Laugh" his gift (a gift which at times turns against him) for rendering the abstract in concrete terms permits him to see evil embodied in the kind of ogre who chases the young at their secret games:

> I shall not forget how his laugh rang out.
> I felt as a fool to have been so caught,
> And checked my steps to make pretence
> It was something among the leaves I sought
> (Though doubtful whether he stayed to see).
> Thereafter I sat me against a tree.

The bathos of this last line proves how truly alien this mode of pseudo-philosophical personifying is to Frost's poetic gifts. Again, in "Pan With Us," even Frost's usual severe and scrupulous craftsmanship fails him when he tries to bring to life, in a New England landscape, a figure from Greek mythology:

> He stood in the zephyr, pipes in hand,
> On a height of native pasture land;
> In all the country he did command
> He saw no smoke and he saw no roof.
> That was well! and he stamped a hoof.

It is hard to believe that this poem appears in the same

volume as the beautifully observed and discreet "Mowing," a poem which shows all Frost's acute powers of perception. It is true, of course, that the scythe in this poem is addressed as though it were a living creature, but here the pathetic fallacy is absolutely acceptable:

That was my long scythe whispering to the ground.
What was it it whispered? I knew not well myself;
Perhaps it was something about the heat of the sun.

What is it, then, about this poem that makes the reader accept willingly the almost anthropomorphic treatment of the scythe, when he resists firmly the personification and presentation of Pan in "Pan With Us"? Perhaps the reason for his acceptance is partly that in "Mowing" the reader is assured of Frost's strong feeling about the scythe, and is, therefore, convinced that he *had* to write his poem in this way; "Pan With Us," on the other hand, seems wholly arbitrary and feels almost as if it were written while the poet was looking the other way. But "Mowing" also demands and holds our complete attention because the reader never for a moment feels that the poet has "a palpable design" upon him or that he is trying to put something across him. There are no tricks in "Mowing", no sleight of hand or mind.

North of Boston,[2] published in 1914, only a year after *A Boy's Will*, shows the thoughtful, meditative Frost, the poet of the dramatic monologue, the inquirer into the drama of nature and natural events. The lyric which celebrates a single emotion is less evident than the more complex poem of scene and human conflict. Already, in a poem such as *A Servant to Servants*, we can hear the quiet but relentless, and now very familiar, tone of Robert Frost:

I didn't make you know how glad I was
To have you come and camp here on our land.
I promised myself to get down some day
And see the way you lived, but I don't know!

Here, Frost has already acquired the ability to use the iambic pentameter as if it were a natural, conversational rhythm. But, apart from its dramatic poems, *North of Boston* is also notable for its adumbration of themes which are later to become peculiarly personal to Frost—fear and foreboding, for example, and a philosophical, stoical unease. Both these themes are reflected at the conclusion of "A Servant to Servants":

> Bless you, of course, you're keeping me from work,
> But, the thing of it is, I *need* to be kept.
> There's work enough to do—there's always that,
> But behind's behind. The worst that you can do
> Is set me back a little more behind.
> I shan't catch up in this world, anyway.
> I'd *rather* you'd not go unless you must.

In this second volume of poems, there is an emphasis on darkness, an emphasis both upon an inward and an outer darkness or blackness, shown here in "Mending Wall" and "The Death of the Hired Man":

> He moves in darkness as it seems to me,
> Not of woods only and the shade of trees.

> When she heard his step,
> She ran on tip-toe down the darkened passage. . . .

Yet two of the best poems in this volume—"Mending Wall" and "After Apple-Picking"—give an almost pulsing life to inanimate objects. They display a feeling for objects as well as a sense of kinship with nature. In a sense, the wall, the byre, the cart, the scythe are as alive to Frost as his men and women, birds and animals, trees and flowers. Yet his response to nature, as the late F. O. Matthiessen pointed out in an unpublished lecture, is entirely realistic; he neither romanticises nature nor loads it with the kind of doomful significance which we find in some of Hardy's poems and novels. Frost seldom indulges at length in the pathetic fallacy even though, somewhat paradoxically perhaps, he often writes about inanimate objects as if they were alive. Thus "Mending Wall," begins:

> Something there is that doesn't love a wall,
> That sends the frozen-ground-swell under it,
> And spills the upper boulders in the sun;
> And makes gaps even two can pass abreast.
> The work of hunters is another thing:
> I have come after them and made repair
> Where they have left not one stone on a stone,
> But they would have the rabbit out of hiding,
> To please the yelping dogs.

Everything here is tangible, concrete; the moral which Frost draws out of his poem ("Good fences make good neighbours") is not arbitrarily imposed but is presented in indirect speech and so has none of the imperiousness which we find where the moral is not drawn out of the subject but clumsily pinned on to it.

Already in *North of Boston* Frost's reticence is manifested, a reticence which springs both from awe and from a fear of the grandiose. He seems to feel instinctively that the vast continent of America is too large, too unknowable, perhaps too alien, to demand from man the kind of relationship which Wordsworth, for example, discovered in the Lake District in England. There is no "nature mysticism" in Frost and little reference to the transcendent. Yet, if he repudiates the grandiose, he does not therefore make needless concessions to the commonplace. His awed reticence produces in his poetry a perfect balance between the natural objects observed and the thoughts and feelings of the observer. This is shown extremely well in "The Wood-Pile," where the delicacy of description is matched by the poet's unwillingness to obtrude himself:

Out walking in the frozen swamp one grey day
I paused and said, "I will turn back from here.
No, I will go on farther—and we shall see."
The hard snow held me, save where now and then
One foot went through. The view was all in lines
Straight up and down of tall slim trees
Too much alike to mark or name a place by
So as to say for certain I was here
Or somewhere else: I was just far from home.
A small bird flew before me. He was careful
To put a tree between us when he lighted, . . .

This poem also contains that element of hesitation, of
indecision about what road to take which appears again
in "The Road Not Taken," the first poem in Frost's next
book, *Mountain Interval*. It is this hesitation which has
provoked Yvor Winters into accusing Frost of being a
"spiritual drifter." It is, on the contrary, the hesitation of
a strong but humble man, a man who pauses before he
makes a decision not because he is pusillanimous but
simply because he is accustomed to weighing up and
considering all his choices, even the simplest ones.

But it is the dramatic poems—"The Mountain,"
"Home Burial," "A Hundred Collars," "Blueberries,"
and "The Code"—which mark the most obvious development in Frost's work as it appears in *North of Boston*. In
such poems as these, he has mastered the difficult art of
handling conversation in verse forms; and these conver-
sations do indeed sound like "the language of ordinary
men", as these extracts from "A Hundred Collars" and
"The Code" illustrate:

"I know him: he's all right. A man's a man.
Separate beds, of course, you understand."

"Something you just now said."
"What did I say?"
               "About our taking pains."

c

"To cock the hay?—because it's going to shower?
I said that more than half an hour ago.
I said it to myself as much as you."

Even when poems like these make use of rhyme, as
"Blueberries" does, the reader seldom feels any awkward-
ness or artificiality. In the dramatic poems and in the
lyrics in *North of Boston*, Frost shows little of that ap-
prentice's clumsiness which we might expect to find in a
poet's second book. This is partly, of course, because he
was not a very young man when his first books were
published, and it may also be that Frost discarded many
of his earliest work-sheets. Nevertheless, his poems are
usually remarkably flawless as far as technique goes;
there are few cracks either in rhythm or verbal texture.
His poetic development, where this can be discerned, lies
rather in the appropriation of new forms and in an in-
creasing subtlety in exploring abstract ideas, than in the
gradual smoothing of what was once rough, or in the
acquisition of dexterity where the poet was at first unsure
of his skill.

Mountain Interval,[3] Frost's third book of poems, begins,
with "The Road Not Taken," one of his best known and
most anthologised poems. *Mountain Interval* contains a
wider variety of poems, and gives a more interesting view
of the mature Frost than *North of Boston*. Nevertheless, it
would be very hard to date accurately many of this poet's
volumes. *Mountain Interval* contains reflective lyrics, such
as "The Road Not Taken," love poems, such as "Meeting
and Passing," narrative poems like "In the Home Stretch"
and "Christmas Trees," and aphoristic-descriptive pieces,
such as "Birches." The general mood of this book is less
sombre than that of *North of Boston*, though Frost's later,
almost habitual stoicism is already apparent in lines like
these from " 'Out, Out' ":

the hand was gone already.
The doctor put him in the dark of ether.

> He lay and puffed his lips out with his breath.
> And then—the watcher at his pulse took fright.
> No one believed. They listened at his heart.
> Little—less—nothing!—and that ended it.
> No more to build on there. And they, since they
> Were not the one dead, turned to their affairs.

This calmness in the face of death is, perhaps, a countryman's prerogative. It is reminiscent of the stark simplicity of John Clare or, in our own time, the directness and bareness of R. S. Thomas. It is not at all that the poet does not feel deeply and painfully, but rather that he never allows his emotions to overwhelm him.

In *Mountain Interval*, there is a poem which was almost completely new for Frost at that time—the beautiful recreation of old age in "An Old Man's Winter Night." In this poem, the poet identifies himself completely with his subject, with the result that his poem, detailed and concrete as it is, is both a reflexion on the condition of being old and also a tender but never sentimental portrait of a particular character. Light and stars are important metaphors in this poem and have something of the *chiaroscuro* effect of brilliance and shading which we find in a Rembrandt painting:

> A light he was to no one but himself
> Where now he sat, concerned with he knew what,
> A quiet light and then not even that.
> He consigned to the moon, such as she was,
> So late-arising, to the broken moon
> As better than the sun in any case
> For such a charge, his snow upon the roof,
> His icicles along the wall to keep. . . .

The precise yet throwaway manner of "consigned" is worth noting here. The same laconic manner and precision are put at the service of human love and compassion in the excellent love poem, "Meeting and Passing" (a poem as fine as any of Frost's later work):

And all the time we talked you seemed to see
Something down there to smile at in the dust.
(Oh it was without prejudice to me!)
Afterward I went past what you had passed
Before we met and you what I had passed.

It has been said that American poets can be more free
and uninhibited in the expression of their own emotional
responses than English poets because they have never had
the emotional liberties of the Georgian movement to
react against. Perhaps Frost, who started writing and
publishing in England at the time of the Georgians, was
instinctively aware of the prevailing over-indulgence in
emotion which usually results in a lack of precision in
language and metaphor. At all events, he could certainly
never be accused of sentimentality. Indeed, his more
personal poems derive much of their power from a sense
of passion being held in check, of deep feeling being
carefully, and not always easily, controlled.

Mountain Interval shows that care for the land and intimacy with natural things which, together with his interest in philosophical and scientific notions, makes Frost a
very individual country poet. There is, in fact, less direct
philosophising in *Mountain Interval* than in some of the
earlier and later books; Frost's eye is here faithfully and
contentedly on the object as this extract from "Range-
Finding" shows:

The battle rent a cobweb diamond-strung
And cut a flower beside a ground bird's nest
Before it stained a single human breast.
The stricken flower bent double and so hung.

This objectivity is also illustrated in " 'Out, Out' ":

The buzz saw snarled and rattled in the yard
And made dust and dropped stove-length sticks of
    wood,
Sweet-scented stuff when the breeze blew across it.

Yet Frost seldom writes a poem that is purely descriptive; his own thoughts or his own personality usually have some part to play even in poems which are mainly concerned with landscape. It is only in those poems where the poet seems to lay too long a shadow over the subject of a given work that we feel his presence to be an obtrusive thing. It is certainly not obtrusive in the slight but accomplished lyric, "The Sound of the Trees," which ends *Mountain Interval*:

> My feet tug at the floor
> And my head sways to my shoulder
> Sometimes when I watch trees sway,
> From the window or the door.

"The Oven Bird," a justly famous poem, is probably one of the most interesting pieces in *Mountain Interval*. In it, the abstract and concrete elements are perfectly blended, the moral implications are recorded but not insisted upon, there is no straining after allegory:

> The bird would cease and be as other birds
> But that he knows in singing not to sing.
> The question that he frames in all but words
> Is what to make of a diminished thing.

Here we can see the power that resides in simple diction when that diction is chosen by a master of language.

There are several love poems in this book; "Bond and Free" makes the comparison between thought and feeling, reason and intuition, which is to become one of Frost's major concerns in his later work. In this comparatively early poem, his attitude remains equivocal and he refuses to commit himself openly:

> His gains in heaven are what they are.
> Yet some say Love by being thrall
> And simply staying possesses all
> In several beauty that Thought fares far
> To find fused in another star.

Frost may not commit himself fully here, yet it is not too difficult to discover where his own allegiances really lie. In "Birches," indeed, he declares "Earth's the right place for love" and goes on to describe his own preference for the immediate, tangible world, and his ability to manage without too much consideration of transcendental things:

> Climb black branches up a snow-white trunk
> *Toward* heaven, till the tree could bear no more,
> But dipped its top and set me down again.
> That would be good both going and coming back.
> One could do worse than be a swinger of branches.

At this point it may be useful to consider just what sort of a poet Frost himself felt he was becoming and hoped to become. How much was he a conscious artist with a clear idea of his future development, with well-conceived blueprints for his growing ambitions? The very fact that Frost has virtually dedicated his whole life to poetry is sufficient proof of his seriousness as an artist. He has not, though, always proved very accessible as a commentator on his own work. Yet his very elusiveness, his fear of taking the mechanism of his own talent to pieces, his reluctance to probe too deeply into the sources of his gift, are indications of the tremendous seriousness of his attitude towards poetry and towards life. In an interview which he gave to *The New Yorker*,[4] he shows how poetry and life are, for him, almost one and the same thing.

> One thing I care about, and I wish young people could care about it, is taking poetry as the first form of understanding. Say it: my *favourite* form of understanding. If poetry isn't understanding all, the whole world, then it isn't worth anything. Young poets forget that poetry must include the mind as well as the emotions. Too many poets delude themselves by thinking the mind is dangerous and must be left out. Well, the mind is dangerous and must be left in.

These last remarks seem to me of extreme importance, for Frost certainly lives up to the precepts which he formulated in this casual interview. Mind is in everything he writes, yet it is never disembodied mind. Ideas fascinate him but they fascinate him because they are the miraculous product of the human brain, not because they have some autonomous or transcendent value of their own. As C. Day Lewis[5] has said:

> Such is the basic design of many of Frost's poems—a kind of argument or dialectic, not imposed upon the subject but worked out in consultation with it. Frost, like any good craftsman, allows the grain of an experience to have a say in the shape of the final product; he takes advice from his material.

Day Lewis has also declared that "Frost found his style young and has not needed to alter it."

Day Lewis's phrase, "not imposed upon the subject but worked out in consultation with it" seems particularly illuminating when applied both to Frost's method of writing and to his general approach to poetry. In a consideration of *Mountain Interval*, it is also useful to remember Auden's remark (quoted by Day Lewis) that Frost's "poems on natural objects . . . are always concerned with them not as foci for mystical meditation or starting points for fantasy, but as things with which and on which man acts in the course of the daily work of gaining a livelihood."

This eye-on-the-object attitude, this respect for the individual person or thing shows itself more forcibly in *Mountain Interval* than in either of Frost's previous books. In this book, it is as if he had not only found his voice and medium, but also discovered the particular territory which is always to be specially his as a writer. Some themes certainly—for example, the spirit-matter dichotomy, and a brooding, sombre concern with man's destiny—are not as yet fully defined, but they are already present in these poems.

As for Frost's voice—that also can be heard at its most characteristic and familiar in this book. And it is, essentially, an American voice; one can almost hear the gentle but decisive New England accent beneath the formal rhythm and occasionally decorous language. This voice is sensed particularly in speeches which are often elliptical, though never really obscure, as this line from "The Vanishing Red" illustrates:

> "Come John," he said, "you want to see the wheel-
> pit?"

The same quality is apparent in "Meeting and Passing":

> Afterward I went past what you had passed
> Before we met and you what I had passed.

This mild form of ellipsis is apparent both in direct and indirect speech in Frost's poems.

In *Mountain Interval*, Frost also shows an ironic interest in machines, and sees them as invaders of the country, spoilers of the land. This viewpoint is shown very clearly in "The Line-Gang":

> Here come the line-gang pioneering by.
> They throw a forest down less cut than broken.
> They plant dead trees for living, and the dead
> They string together with a living thread. . . .
>
> With a laugh,
> An oath of towns that set the wild at naught
> They bring the telephone and telegraph.

"Hyla Brook" probably expresses most completely Frost's steadfast and enduring beliefs; it is interesting that in this poem too, as in so many others, he protects his personal feelings by using the plural "we":

> A brook to none but who remember long.
> This as it will be seen is other far

Than with brooks taken otherwhere in song.
We love the things we love for what they are.

With his next volume of poems, entitled *New Hampshire*,[6] Robert Frost may be said to be completely at ease as a poet. In this book, the range is wide, the manner assured and the subject-matter subtle and deeply felt. *New Hampshire* contains, among other poems, the long title poem, "A Star in a Stone-Boat," "The Star-Splitter," "The Witch of Coös," "Fragmentary Blue," "Fire and Ice," "To E. T.," "Stopping by Woods on a Snowy Evening," "For Once, Then, Something," "Two Look at Two," "Looking for a Sunset Bird in Winter," and "The Need of Being Versed in Country Things." Indeed, this volume contains some of Frost's best and most mature work. Yet the poetry here grows naturally and easily out of that in *Mountain Interval*; there are no sudden reversals of taste, no extreme experiments in verse forms or rhythms. And the poet is interested in precisely the same subjects and themes which concerned him in the previous book. There is no slickness or glibness here, no over-familiarity with a subject or a terrain; there is only that most valuable and lasting quality of every major poet—an acknowledged and accepted awareness of power.

New Hampshire shows, too, how fortunate a poet is when he has found a country, a poetic material, and a way of life which give him every possible opportunity of exercising his poetic gift. One never feels with Frost (as one does perhaps with Pound and Stevens) that the English language and the whole past tradition of English poetry are inadequate for his purposes. He has enriched that tradition, but he has never altered it radically. Frost had to find his own voice, but he did not need to discover a language; it was already waiting for him.

The title poem of this book shows Frost at his most relaxed. In blank verse, he surveys the states of New

Hampshire and Vermont and the people who live there:

> Anything I can say about New Hampshire
> Will serve almost as well about Vermont,
> Excepting that they differ in their mountains.
> The Vermont mountains stretch extended straight;
> New Hampshire mountains curl up in a coil.

This is a style that is as apt for description as for conversation; it rolls off the tongue. The form is extraordinarily flexible, subservient to any mood—for example, the reflective,

> The more the sensibilitist I am
> the more I seem to want my mountains wild.

and the colloquial,

> we heard him say
> On coming nearer: "Wasn't she an *i*-deal
> Son-of-a-bitch."

But Frost can also be formal and decorous, as in the three-line rhyming stanzas of "A Star in a Stone-Boat." This poem, incidentally, shows once again Frost's obsession with astronomy:

> From following walls I never lift my eye
> Except at night to places in the sky
> Where showers of charted meteors let fly.

The same interest is displayed in the blank verse "The Star-Splitter":

> We spread our two legs as we spread its three,
> Pointed our thoughts the way we pointed it. . . .

Frost is talking here about a telescope; the phrase, "pointed our thoughts," is typical of the way he handles immaterial things in physical terms, reminding us of Donne who also had this gift for gripping an abstraction with metaphorical language.

"The Axe-Helve" and "The Grindstone" in this book

are both poems of description, but in the former, Frost wraps his feeling for country tools in a simple narrative. This is one of his most familiar *genres*, the kind of poem by which he is often best known. "Two Witches" ("The Witch of Coös" and "The Pauper Witch of Grafton") shows Frost identifying himself with one particular country superstition—a belief in magic. In the dialogue between the Mother and the Son in "The Witch of Coös," he achieves a remarkable eeriness simply by means of repetition:

> Son. We think they had a grave down in the cellar.
> Mother. We know they had a grave down in the cellar.

"The Pauper Witch of Grafton" is less celebrated than the first witch piece but it is a better poem. In the form of a dramatic monologue, Frost shows how completely he can lose himself in his subject. The moraliser, the observer, the lyric poet have vanished and we are left simply with the fact of the witch with her threats and prophecies:

> Well, I showed Arthur Amy signs enough
> Off from the house as far as we could keep. . . .

The last, stoic lines of the poem are particularly fine:

> You *can* come down from everything to nothing.
> All is, if I'd a-known when I was young
> And full of it, that this would be the end,
> It doesn't seem as if I'd had the courage
> To make so free and kick up in folks' faces,
> I might have, but it doesn't seem as if.

That laconic, almost broken-off last line is extremely effective. Writing of this part of the poem, Randall Jarrell[7] has remarked how "the testy, acrid mockery of the old pauper, of the 'noted witch' always plagued by an adulterous generation for a sign, turns into something very different as she remembers the man who first exposed and then married her."

New Hampshire shows Frost in almost every mood; it contains "Fire and Ice," an extremely personal short lyric:

> I think I know enough of hate
> To say that for destruction ice
> Is also great
> And would suffice.

The same direct voice also speaks in "To E. T.," the poem written for Edward Thomas. But even when he is most personal, Frost is never mawkish or embarrassing. He draws the reader into his own feelings, but he will not let him wallow in them, any more than he wallows in them himself. And, of course, the emotion is all the more moving when it is controlled by such a "firm restraint."

"Fragmentary Blue" is remarkably like a number of Wallace Stevens's poems, particularly the second of the two stanzas:

> Since earth is earth, perhaps, not heaven (as yet)—
> Though some savants make earth include the sky;
> And blue so far above us comes so high,
> It only gives our wish for blue a whet.

This chance similarity to Stevens's style is, however, a very superficial thing. The likenesses are only present in the poetic properties and the odd word ("savants," for example); where Stevens would use the occasion for a reflexion on the relations between imagination and reality, Frost is more interested in our reactions to the sky simply as we see it. There is certainly thought in Frost's poem, but the thought is little more than a vivid observation. With Stevens, a whole metaphysical system would have been laid before us.

"For Once, Then, Something" makes an interesting comparison with "Fragmentary Blue" because it shows another approach to the pleasure which natural objects can give simply because they are finite and limited:

One drop fell from a fern, and lo, a ripple
Shook whatever it was lay there at bottom,
Blurred it, blotted it out. What was that whiteness?
A truth? A pebble of quartz? For once, then, some-
     thing.

This tentative statement is characteristic of Frost's
continual refusal to make large claims, to strain after
meanings or analogies. In many ways, he is the least
symbolist of poets—far less of one, indeed, than Wordsworth who forced loads of metaphysical significance upon
his clouds, lakes, and mountains. Randall Jarrell,[8] when
discussing "Design," a later poem, has commented on
"an exaggeratedly physical and literally astronomical
view of things [which] is so common, and so unremarked
on, in Frost." He has also referred to the "longing,
tenderness, and passive sadness" in Frost's work, and to
the poet's obsessive themes "of isolation, of extinction,
and of the final limitation of man."

But Frost's poems are seldom totally sombre, certainly
not the majority of those which appear in *New Hampshire*.
There is a deep and pervasive delight in the beautiful
love poem, "Two Look at Two":

    "This *must* be all." It was all. Still they stood,
    A great wave from it going over them,
    As if the world in one unlooked-for favour
    Had made them certain earth returned their love.

It is the miraculous simplicity, the bare statement, that
holds the imagination in a poem like this—and Frost has
written dozens of poems as good. He has that tact, that
reticence which only the major poet knows, instinctively,
when to employ.

The same control over rhetoric (when the poet might,
surely, be tempted to indulge in the rhetorical or grandiose) is also apparent in the last poem in this book, "The
Need of Being Versed in Country Things." The poem is
about a derelict barn, but Frost uses the subject and the

occasion to write a poem about the alliance between
sensitivity and acceptance, the realistic attitude which is
essential to the true countryman. And, of course, the
poem is concerned with far more than just this; it
reverbrates far beyond its immediate subject. It is
profoundly simple and, likewise, simply profound:

> The birds that came to it through the air
> At broken windows flew out and in,
> Their murmur more like the sigh we sigh
> From too much dwelling on what has been.
>
> Yet for them the lilac renewed its leaf,
> And the aged elm, though touched with fire;
> And the dry pump flung upon awkward arm;
> And the fence post carried a strand of wire.
>
> For them there was really nothing sad.
> But though they rejoiced in the nest they kept,
> One had to be versed in country things
> Not to believe the phoebes wept.

In this poem, Frost has struck a perfect balance
between the attitude of the observer and commentator
and the complete immersion of his own personality. He is
most deeply present in his subject, and profoundly moved
by it. "The sigh we sigh" includes the poet, the reader,
and all humanity. Yet everything in the poem is pared
down to precision and simplicity. As Randall Jarrell[9]
says of "The Need of Being Versed in Country Things":

> ... I am not only left helpless to say whether this is
> slight or not, I don't even want to know: I am too sure
> of what I have even to want to say what it is, so that I
> will say if you ask me, as St. Augustine did about time:
> "I know if you don't ask me."

Jarrell's feelings about this poem are perfectly under-
standable; nevertheless, it is entirely amenable to analysis,
though it certainly does not need much explication.

Robert Fitzgerald[10] has made some general remarks

about Frost which seem to be pertinent at this point, in a study of the poet's contribution to modern literature. Defying Yvor Winters's fierce strictures, Fitzgerald declares,

> That stern critic, Yvor Winters, considers Frost an Emersonian and therefore untrustworthy sage; but he would probably concede that on occasion Frost has had a harder edge and eye than Emerson, more humour, and more of the fear of God. It would be going too far to think of him as a religious poet, but his work tends towards wholeness, and thus towards catholicism at heart.

What Fitzgerald means by "wholeness," is quite clear and it is, perhaps, the volume entitled *New Hampshire* which first shows Frost at home with his full powers. The sheer exultant energy in this book, the assurance, delight, and skill with many different poetic forms are clearly displayed here. In later poems, Frost may go more deeply and more darkly into his overriding themes, preoccupations, and obsessions, but *New Hampshire* shows us at least the adumbrations of his finest later work. Nothing could surprise us after we have read this book—and nothing could surprise us simply because anything and everything now seem possible to this poet.

One of the most amiable and also one of the most hopeful things about this volume is Frost's willingness to admit the strange, the frightening, the foreboding. His poetic skill is quite definitely at its height here, but this does not mean that his poems give easy or glib answers to man's predicament on this earth, or to the poet's personal problems. What makes this book so satisfying is what Keats called the poet's "negative capability," his readiness to be in doubt rather than to find tidy solutions or simple answers. The poem called "A Boundless Moment" displays Frost's intelligently humble attitude particularly well; the poem begins

He halted in the wind, and—what was that
Far in the maples, pale, but not a ghost?
He stood there bringing March against his thought,
And yet too ready to believe the most.

"Oh, that's the Paradise-in-bloom," I said;
And truly it was fair enough for flowers
Had we but in us to assume in March
Such white luxuriance as May for ours.

New Hampshire answers, indirectly, many questions, but it also poses the problem of the poet's attitude to nature, his relationship with the soil: the dialectic, in fact, between natural growing things and the poet's own reasonings. There is a sense in which the fact of being labelled a "nature poet" may be said to protect the poet from too much ratiocination, too much introspection; a life lived close to the land is, after all, essentially an extrovert and active life. Frost's attitude to the land is not as simple as this. He is a representative of a more subtle, more tormented school of poets. He combines the questioning of Wordsworth with the tortured self-awareness of Clare or R. S. Thomas. Thinking is in everything that he writes, yet he has never allowed cold thinking to have the last word. This conflict between thought and action is at the very heart of Frost's poetry. It certainly accounts for his comparatively few failures, but it is also undoubtedly responsible for his many large and triumphant successes. Abstractions haunt him but they are never exorcised except by the concrete image, the living word.

REFERENCES

1. *C.P.*, p. 25.
2. *C.P.*, p. 53.
3. *C.P.*, p. 129.
4. *W.D.*, p. 69.
5. *R.F.*, p. 13.
6. *C.P.*, p. 185.
7. *P.A.*, p. 62.
8. *P.A.*, p. 53.
9. *P.A.*, p. 68
10. *New Republic*, 8 Aug. 1949, p. 18.

CHAPTER III

WEST-RUNNING BROOK,
A FURTHER RANGE,
A WITNESS TREE

In *West-Running Brook*,[1] published in 1928, there is a poem related to religion which is far less equivocal than most of Frost's "religious" poems. It is called "Sitting By a Bush in Broad Sunlight" and it is a brief lyric about the changes which religion has undergone since the Ages of Faith. It ends,

> God once declared he was true
> And then took the veil and withdrew,
> And remember how final a hush
> Then descended of old on the bush.
>
> God once spoke to people by name.
> The sun once imparted its flame.
> One impulse persists as our breath;
> The other persists as our faith.

Frost here sees the world as a place from which God has withdrawn all obvious signs of himself. Yet his approach to religion is not a mystical one; he does not pursue God through prayer, penance and suffering, nor does he declare, as Hopkins declared, that "The world is charged with the grandeur of God." There are certainly poems in which Frost demonstrates that the order and symmetry of the world must be dependent on something more pervasive and more powerful than mere chance: but, on the whole, his poems tend to show the dialectic between chance and pattern, between impulse and reason. In

D

these matters, Frost is usually tentative rather than didactic. In his more philosophical poems, he appears to be stating one position out of many possible others, rather than laying claim to one exclusive truth. Thus the menacing quality in "Once by the Pacific," another poem in *West-Running Brook*, is due as much to the poet's refusal to organise the scene round one central, philosophical position, as to the threat implicit in the natural objects which the scene contains:

> It looked as if a night of dark intent
> Was coming, and not only a night, an age.
> Someone had better be prepared for rage.
> There would be more than ocean-water broken
> Before God's last *Put out the Light* was spoken.

"It looked as if," "Someone had better . . ."—these words and phrases suggest not the pusillanimity of the spiritual drifter, but the profound probings and inquiries of a mind which is too tough and too eager to be able to accept a total agnosticism. Frost will not say "I am certain of nothing," but, on the other hand, neither will he say, "I am certain of everything." This fact is central to his whole attitude to life, and it also produces the tension in his best poems.

But *West-Running Brook*, Frost's fifth book of poems, also shows the extension of many other ranges of interest and preoccupation. His obsession with astronomy is again apparent in "On Looking Up By Chance At the Constellations":

> You'll wait a long, long time for anything much
> To happen in heaven beyond the floats of cloud
> And the Northern Lights that run like tingling
>   nerves. . . .

> We may as well go patiently on with our life,
> And look elsewhere than to stars and moon and sun
> For the shocks and changes we need to keep us sane.

If Frost's usual attitude to life is a stoical, acquiescent one, this poem, nevertheless, makes it clear that natural events and objects can never be a mere escape for him, an excuse for meditation or a proffering of consolation. He is as stern with nature as he is with himself, and when he *is* compassionate, his compassion springs from full knowledge and a sense of reality, not from softness or sentimentality. As he says in a short poem called "Devotion":

> The heart can think of no devotion
> Greater than being shore to the ocean—
> Holding the curve of one position,
> Counting an endless repetition.

But the poems in *West-Running Brook* are by no means restricted to those concerned with religious or philosophical reflexion. Frost's visual sense is, in this book, as lively as ever, his grasp of the apt metaphor as exciting and surprising as in any of the earlier books. With every book, his control over language and imagery is becoming more exultant. "Spring Pools" is as fine as any poem he had written previously, and it has that taut, bare quality, which never becomes either strained or affected, that is peculiarly personal to Frost's later tone of voice and way of looking at things:

> The trees that have it in their pent-up buds
> To darken nature and be summer woods—
> Let them think twice before they use their powers
> To blot out and drink up and sweep away
> These flowery waters and these watery flowers
> From snow that melted only yesterday.

The use of the pathetic fallacy ("Let them think twice . . .") in this poem is entirely acceptable to the reader, partly because Frost does not force it to bear too much weight of meaning, and partly because it is used so lightly and directly that the reader never for a moment supposes that Frost believes that trees really have the power of thought. His bold admonition to the trees is not in any sense an attempt to make them appear human; the pathetic fallacy is for Frost simply another kind of metaphor.

This literary device is again employed in "Acceptance," where a bird is given some words which seem to be particularly Frostian in significance. They embody a mood, rather than a prevailing attitude—in this case, the mood of passivity, of letting be, of not wishing to interfere:

> At most he thinks or twitters softly, "Safe!
> Now let the night be dark for all of me.
> Let the night be too dark for me to see
> Into the future. Let what will be, be."

It is unwise to impute to a poet all the ideas which are expressed by other characters in his verse; however, in Frost's case, even though his lyrics and narrative poems contain many different ideas and attitudes, these ideas and attitudes often represent various aspects of the same thing. The poet, in fact, is using verse to probe for meaning, but his ideas are not imposed on the poetry; they emerge from it, except in a few contrived and awkward poems.

West-Running Brook also contains "Acquainted With the Night," perhaps Frost's most widely known poem—it certainly appears in practically every American anthology for schools. The most interesting thing about this poem is its supreme and calculated reticence, its insistence on understatement, its refusal to say more than the poet thinks or feels. In this, it is typically Frostian; in another sense it is rather uncharacteristic; it shows Frost simply setting a scene, and rejecting the opportunity to draw a moral or a conclusive statement from it. The resonance and power of the poem reside entirely in its implications, in the possibilities of interpretation which the poet lays before the reader. It is a non-committal poem, but it is by no means an indecisive one. The firm tread of the rhyming five-foot lines reflects the firm thought of the poet, his resolve not to be swayed one way or the other by the suggestiveness of the scene. In short, Frost displays here the "negative capability," that decision to rest among uncertainties and not to draw dogmas too easily out of deeply felt personal experiences. If this is what Yvor Winters means by "spiritual drifting," then it is a very stark and dedicated sort of drifting which Frost practises:

> I have stood still and stopped the sound of feet
> When far away an interrupted cry
> Came over houses from another street,
>
> But not to call me back or say goodbye;
> And further still at an unearthly height,
> One luminary clock against the sky
>
> Proclaimed the time was neither wrong nor right.
> I have been one acquainted with the night.

In hands less assured than Frost's, this might seem a rather histrionic, even a slightly affected poem. However, when Frost declares "I have been one acquainted with the night," he is not laying claim to a sense of darkness and deprivation which is unknown to other men; he is neither making a defiant gesture nor seeking comfort. He is simply describing, with immense restraint, a mood which is well-known to all men and women of sensibility and with inquiring minds.

"Acquainted With the Night" makes an interesting comparison with the poem "Desert Places," which appears in Frost's next book; in this later poem, the poet is describing a similar mood and situation but makes a more intimately personal analysis of it:

> I have it in me so much nearer home
> To scare myself with my own desert places.

To make such a naked confession as this and, at the same time, to avoid self-pity completely shows how closely Frost's poetic skill is bound up with his integrity as a man.

The title poem of *West-Running Brook* contains some of Frost's most frequently repeated opinions and attitudes. Characteristically, he puts these ideas into the mouth of a fictitious person. Thus, in the following lines, he considers what is almost an obsession with him—the play of and the tug between various opposites in the world:

> "Speaking of contraries, see how the brook
> In that white wave runs counter to itself.
> It is from that in water we were from
> Long, long before we were from any creature. . . .
>
> The universal cataract of death
> That spends to nothingness—and unresisted,
> Save by some strange resistance in itself,
> Not just a swerving, but a throwing back,
> As if regret were in it and were sacred.
> It has this throwing backward on itself
> So that the fall of most of it is always
> Raising a little, sending up a little.
> Our life runs down in sending up the clock.
> The brook runs down in sending up our life. . . .
>
> It is this backward motion toward the source,
> Against the stream, the most we see ourselves in. . . ."

This lucid, balanced verse is a perfect vehicle for philosophical argument and bare statement. Here, Frost, using the general "we," commits himself more deeply than he does in many of his overtly personal lyrics. This is the poet talking of his own struggles and conflicts. The *persona* who is speaking for him is a thin disguise; the processes of thought are Frost's alone. The movement of his mind among many provisional answers to the meaning of life is not a restless activity or a dilettante taking-up of one attitude after another, but a steady advance, a scrutiny which becomes more searching as the poet grows older. But the really interesting thing is that it is *through* poetry that Frost examines various philosophical positions, and also makes his metaphysical discoveries. In this sense, but in this sense only, he resembles Edwin Muir.

In *West-Running Brook*, the poems are almost equally distributed in type between tentative, descriptive lyrics, and narratives or arguments in verse. The former type can sometimes be almost naïve both in statement and content; "Bereft" is a fair example:

> Something sinister in the tone
> Told me my secret must be known:
> Word I was in the house alone
> Somehow must have gotten abroad,
> Word I was in my life alone,
> Word I had no one left but God.

The tone of this poem is undoubtedly sincere and perhaps it only seems naïve when it is compared with some of the more complicated and sophisticated poems in *West-Running Brook*. Naïveté which, by the end of a very short lyric, has developed into a muscular subtlety, is also evident in "Tree at My Window":

> But, tree, I have seen you taken and tossed,
> And if you have seen me when I slept,
> You have seen me when I was taken and swept
> And all but lost.
>
> That day she put our heads together,
> Fate had her imagination about her,
> Your head so much concerned with outer,
> Mine with inner, weather.

Frost seldom permits himself much introspection in the conventional sense; he refers to it in passing far more often than he examines the findings of his own inner searchings.

"The Lovely Shall be Choosers" is rather different from most of the other poems in *West-Running Brook*. It is a poem about a woman and, unlike most of Frost's other portraits, it is an account of the kind of woman Frost would wish to exist, rather than a description of the person this woman actually is:

> "Do it by joys, and leave her always blameless.
> Be her first joy her wedding,
> That though a wedding,
> Is yet—well something they know, he and she.
> That though she grieves, her grief is secret."

In Frost's next book of poems, *A Further Range*,[2] there is a poem called "Provide, Provide" about which Randall Jarrell[3] has declared enthusiastically, "I was floating in a quarry with my chin on a log when I first discovered that I knew 'Provide, Provide' by heart. . . ." This poem is very like a spell or an incantation; it is far less explicit and more enigmatic than any of Frost's earlier poems. It is a riddle, an admonition and a conjuration:

> Some have relied on what they knew;
> Others on being simply true.
> What worked for them might work for you.
>
> No memory of having starred
> Atones for later disregard,
> Or keeps the end from being hard.
>
> Better to go down dignified
> With boughten friendship at your side
> Than none at all. Provide, provide!

These lines appear to be a warning to the reader to lay up even the most unworthy earthly treasure for himself, and they illustrate all Frost's resourcefulness with language and all his verbal brilliance; the rhymes fall expectedly yet without that monotonous "click" which reveals a poem's mechanism and therefore spoils its total design. The first three lines of the poem, with their haunting, magical quality, prepare the reader for the aphorisms which are to come:

> The witch that came (the withered hag)
> To wash the steps with pail and rag,
> Was once the beauty Abishag. . . .

Another poem in *A Further Range* also demands detailed examination simply because it also has this haunting, laconic quality, a quality which is relatively new in Frost's work at this time. It is called "Neither Out Far Nor In Deep" and it ends

> The land may vary more;
> But whatever the truth may be—
> The water comes ashore,
> And the people look at the sea.
>
> They cannot look out far.
> They cannot look in deep.
> But when was that ever a bar
> To any watch they keep?

This poem needs a little analysis on the level of mere meaning. Its message is explicit, its metaphor perfectly appropriate to the admonition the poet wishes it to convey. And, as so often with Frost's work, what appears superficially to be allegory turns out to be a metaphor chosen for its directness and fittingness; the metaphor carries the meaning. It does not, as allegory does, change it into something else or transfer the meaning to another level.

It is hard to believe that *A Further Range* originally appeared in 1936. From the beginning, Frost appears to have had that ease, but never slickness, with language and technique which has always enabled him to find the almost stunningly right conclusion to a poem. Some critics have thought that Frost is too simple a poet, that the content of his verse is sometimes crude and obvious. One could cite and quote dozens of poems which would quickly refute this shallow judgment. "Design," from *A Further Range*, would certainly be a good example. In this poem, Frost considers the appearance of order in the natural world, and hints at the probable cause of this order. His method is tentative yet affirmative. The poem, merely by asking questions, manages to reveal the reality and importance of design and pattern:

> What had that flower to do with being white,
> The wayside blue and innocent heal-all?
> What brought the kindred spider to that height,
> Then steered the white moth thither in the night?
> What but design of darkness to appall?—
> If design govern in a thing so small.

The splendid penultimate line of this poem reminds us of the dark side of Frost's imagination, his obsession with pain and evil (though the obsession is entirely free from masochism). We are reminded once more how the stars are a prevailing theme with Frost, both as a fact and as a metaphor. They symbolise light and order, peace and tranquillity. In every book he has written, there is either a whole poem or parts of a poem devoted to the stars. The most poignant appearance of stars in *A Further Range*— and here they are accepted stoically by the poet, rather than looked to for consolation—is at the end of the beautiful "Desert Places":

> They cannot scare me with their empty spaces
> Between stars—on stars where no human race is.
> I have it in me so much nearer home
> To scare myself with my own desert places.

A Further Range also contains a few brief rhymed thoughts or aphorisms which are new to Frost's work.

These verses are humorous rather than witty; fair examples of them are the following from "Precaution":

> I never dared be radical when young
> For fear it would make me conservative when old.

and from "The Span of Life":

> The old dog barks backward without getting up.
> I can remember when he was a pup.

These lines lack any sparkling sophistication, and in them Frost does, for once, appear rather simplicist in attitude. There is something truly homespun about these clumsy attempts at the epigram. They provoke a mild laugh but were, surely, scarcely worth printing in a serious book of poems. But *A Further Range* also includes many poems whose combination of psychological perception and visual imagination makes them easily recognisable as the work of Robert Frost. "Two Tramps in Mud Time" is a graphic example of this *genre*. The last stanza of this poem is a direct statement of Frost's conflicts as a man and as a poet, of the dialectic between his "avocation" and "vocation":

> But yield who will to their separation,
> My object in living is to unite
> My avocation and my vocation
> As my two eyes make one in sight.
> Only where love and need are one,
> And the work is play for mortal stakes,
> Is the deed ever really done
> For Heaven and the future's sakes.

Here, as in many of his earlier poems, Frost invokes Heaven: but the reader is by no means sure whether this Heaven is an orthodox Christian one or simply a cipher for some desirable state of existence which Frost can imagine, even if he cannot accept it as an objective fact. And, of course, "Heaven" here may well be just another name for God. But the world Frost gives his fullest credence to is the physical one, the world of sensible objects—not a transcendent one. He is as far from being a Platonist as any philosophically-inclined poet can well be. Yet, on the other hand, he is never merely a materialist. Perhaps the enigmatic quality of so much of Frost's later work arises from his insistence upon the perfect unity of solid matter and spiritual essence. The dilemma which is necessarily produced by such a view is well expressed in *A Further Range* in "The White-Tailed Hornet":

> As long on earth
> As our comparisons were stoutly upward
> With gods and angels, we were men at least,
> But little lower than the gods and angels.
> But once comparisons were yielded downward,
> Once we began to see our images
> Reflected in the mud and even dust,
> 'Twas disillusion upon disillusion.

Frost's verse is formal, even, at times, stately; its movements are often easily anticipated. Yet, despite this, his technique is so flexible, his handling of language and cadence so careful and delicate, that he is able to give his most elegant poems the air of spontaneity. His ideas thus appear not as preconceived notions, but as sudden discoveries. His best poetry conveys the very processes of thought and speculation. Although Frost's finest work does give this impression of the mind in the act of working, there are still poems in *A Further Range* which present him in a more conventional mood, though by no means in an uninteresting one. "At Woodward's Gardens" shows him in a more didactic frame of mind than any of the other poems in this book do. It ends,

> Who said it mattered
> What monkeys did or didn't understand?
> They might not understand a burning-glass.

They might not understand the sun itself.
It's knowing what to do with things that counts.

This is Frost at his most stubbornly schoolmasterish
and also, perhaps, at his most unattractive. There is no
subtlety here, no self-questioning, no doubt. We prefer a
poet, even the greatest, when he is least assured about
things, when his confidence is tempered by self-distrust
and by indecision. It is not that vacillation is in itself
poetically appealing, but rather that too overt an assertion, too knowledgeable and assured an attitude destroys
that element in all poetry which is, perhaps, the most
satisfying and lasting: I mean an attitude of mind which
can ask questions and, by simply asking, make a complete poetic statement.

My criticism of the didactic element in Frost, however,
is only relevant to a comparatively small part of his
complete *oeuvre*, and certainly applies only to a very small
portion of the poems in *A Further Range*. At their best, his
poems present and enact a mood, a scene, a season, an
experience; in his most integrated poems, his comments
arise serenely and inevitably out of the subject-matter of
the given poem. The following examples are instances of
this integration in two of the poems in *A Further Range*,
"The Strong are Saying Nothing" and "To a Thinker":

Wind goes from farm to farm in wave on wave,
And carries no cry of what is hoped to be.
There may be little or much beyond the grave,
But the strong are saying nothing until they see.

I own I never really warmed
To the reformer or reformed.
And yet conversion has its place
Not halfway down the scale of grace.
So if you find you must repent
From side to side in argument,
At least don't use your mind too hard,
But trust my instinct—I'm a bard.

This last quotation has laid Frost open to a good deal of
criticism on the score that he distrusts thought and lays
too much stress on instinct and insight. Yvor Winters is
not the only critic who has made such charges against
Frost. Yet a thorough and calm reading of almost any of
Frost's books will indicate just how wide of the mark such
accusations are. In *A Further Range*, there is a long poem
called "Build Soil—A Political Pastoral." Here Frost
shows just how keenly his mind works; yet his arguments
are presented in a purely poetic form (blank verse), a
form which seems perfectly suited to the subject:

> come close, let us conspire—
> In self-restraint, if in restraint of trade.
> You will go to your run-out mountain farm
> And do what I command you. I take care
> To command only what you meant to do
> Anyway. That is my style of dictator.
> Build soil. Turn the farm in upon itself
> Until it can contain itself no more,
> But sweating-full, drips wine and oil a little.

This poem reminds us more of Browning's monologues
than of any prose political pamphleteering. The language
is less taut and nervous than it is in Frost's lyrics, and the
statements made lack the overtones which we find in his
shorter pieces. Yet the iambic pentameter in this
"Political Pastoral" is a perfect vehicle for what Frost
has to say; it is flexible, varied and sinuous.

If *A Further Range* is lacking in the virtuosity of some of
Frost's other books, it is, nonetheless, a thoroughly
satisfactory collection. It marks that consolidation of a
talent, that sense of a poet both adapting himself to a
number of new ideas and easing himself gently into some
new poetic forms. The obvious successes in this book—
"Desert Places," "Design," "Provide, Provide,"—are as
fine and as reverberant as any of Frost's previous work. *A
Further Range* also makes it perfectly clear that Frost is

fundamentally a traditional poet who nevertheless knows that revolutions, whether literary or political, are an important part of life. He is certainly not one of the great, modern, American poetic innovators, but there is no doubt at all that the litheness of his rhythm, the spare brilliance of his language, the stark simplicity and directness of his imagery are an integral part of his work because the poems so clearly reflect the character of the man who wrote them. They are also present, however, because Frost has been influenced, in however indirect a way, by that paring down to simplicity and perfection which was the chief aim of the obvious experimentalists of this century, such as Pound and Eliot. Like Yeats—whom he resembles in scarcely any other way—Frost is an original, a writer who has used traditional methods and approaches for his own ends; and like Yeats again, he has never felt the need to do violence to these methods.

Frost's next book, *A Witness Tree*,[4] contains some of his most flawless lyrics. Indeed, with three exceptions, this book is entirely composed of short poems. "The Silken Tent," is, perhaps, the finest of all Frost's love poems. It is warm, tender, highly wrought yet entirely devoid of artificiality or rhetoric. It is a poem of love and admiration, rather than one of passion, and it is only possible to reveal the sure craftsmanship of it, the complete triumph of a masterly simplicity, by quoting the sonnet entire:

> She is as in a field a silken tent
> At midday when a sunny summer breeze
> Has dried the dew and all its ropes relent,
> So that in guys it gently sways at ease,
> And its supporting central cedar pole,
> That is its pinnacle to heavenward
> And signifies the sureness of the soul,
> Seems to owe naught to any single cord,
> But strictly held by none, is loosely bound
> By countless silken ties of love and thought

> To everything on earth the compass round,
> And only by one's going slightly taut
> In the capaciousness of summer air
> Is of the slightest bondage made aware.

A Witness Tree also contains "Never Again Would
Birds' Song be the Same," another sonnet celebrating the
beauty of a particular woman:

> Moreover her voice upon their voices crossed
> Had now persisted in the woods so long
> That probably it never would be lost.
> Never again would birds' song be the same.
> And to do that to birds was why she came.

This poem makes an interesting comparison with Wallace
Stevens's "The Idea of Order at Key West":

> She sang beyond the genius of the sea.
> The water never formed to mind or voice,
> Like a body wholly body, fluttering
> Its empty sleeves; and yet its mimic motion
> Made constant cry, caused constantly a cry,
> That was not ours although we understood,
> Inhuman, of the veritable ocean.

The verbal similarities between these two poems serve to
emphasise the essential differences between Frost and
Stevens rather than the likenesses. Where Stevens is
abstract, impersonal and metaphysical, Frost is concrete,
personal and factual. The woman in Stevens's poem is
simply an opportunity for the poet to continue his lifelong dialectic between reality and the imagination.
Frost's woman is known and discovered through love;
she is a person, an individual, not a concept or a cipher.
   But these are not value judgments. Both these important poets are American, yet Stevens is also cosmopolitan;
in particular, he has learnt from the art and literature of
France. Frost, however, is deep-rootedly American, even

though he started his life as a poet in England. F. O. Matthiessen[5] has put this whole matter very cogently:

> Twenty-five years old by the turn of the century, Frost still belongs to the older America. . . . Frost has voiced a naturalistic faith, which has not always escaped complacence, and Eliot's return to orthodoxy has never quite surmounted the somber weariness of doubt.

There is much truth in this statement, though I do not believe that a full and searching reading of Frost's work would reveal any complacency in it; there is far more conflict than Matthiessen is willing to admit.

In speaking of Frost as a "naturalistic" poet, one must always be wary of missing the subtlety and sophistication of his best work. His stark simplicities are the simplicities a man finds after much experience and a great deal of painful self-questioning. The following powerful and direct statement, which appears in *A Witness Tree* in a poem called "The Most Of It," could only have been written by a man who has thought, studied and observed for a very long time:

> Some morning from the boulder-broken beach
> He would cry out on life, that what it wants
> Is not its own love back in copy speech,
> But counter love, original response.

This is a passionate protest, and "The Most Of It" ends on a grim and haunting note; this is indeed what Stevens called "the poem of the act of the mind":

> As a great buck it powerfully appeared,
> Pushing the crumpled water up ahead,
> And landed pouring like a waterfall,
> And stumbled through the rocks with horny tread,
> And forced the underbrush—and that was all.

E

Randall Jarrell[6] has made some general remarks about Frost which seem to be particularly relevant to this poem;

> Frost is that rare thing, a complete or representative poet, and not one of the brilliant or partial poets who do justice, far more than justice, to a portion of reality, and leave the rest of things forlorn. When you know Frost's poems you know surprisingly well how the world seemed to one man, and what it was to seem that way: the great *Gestalt* that each of us makes from himself and all that isn't himself is very clear, very complicated, very contradictory in the poetry. The grimness and awfulness and untouchable sadness of things, both in the world and in the self, have justice done to them in the poems, but no more justice than is done to the tenderness and love and delight. . . . If some of the poems come out of a cynical common sense that is only wisdom's backward shadow, others come out of wisdom itself. . . . If we compare this wisdom with, say, that of the last of the Old Ones, Goethe, we are saddened and frightened at how much the poet's scope has narrowed, at how difficult and partial and idiosyncratic the application of his intelligence has become, at what terrible sacrifices he has had to make in order to avoid making others still more terrible.

> Yet in Frost, we rediscover that completeness and all-inclusiveness of vision which is only possible to a poet humble enough not to want to alter a tradition radically, and tough and original enough to make something entirely his own out of a received language and a literary inheritance. There is no doubt that in his most profound poems, Frost not only presents a world but also shares with us the feeling of actually discovering it. And he is able to do this largely because tradition for him is not simply a literary matter. He expresses his feeling for America, its land, its pre-history and its history, in "The

Gift Outright" (also in *A Witness Tree*). Here he speaks of the intimate relationship between men and their country:

> Such as we were we gave ourselves outright
> (The deed of gift was many deeds of war)
> To the land vaguely realizing westward,
> But still unstoried, artless, unenhanced,
> Such as she was, such as she would become.

The problems of being an American, and particularly of being an American poet or novelist, have for some time now been one of the chief subjects of interest and discussion among writers in the United States. Frost faces these problems too, but he does not restrict the predicament to Americans; what some writers and sociologists have seen as a peculiarly American dilemma—namely, the isolation of man in a country that still has its past to fashion—is viewed by him as a universal situation, a general loneliness. Many of his poems are about this very sense of isolation. Sometimes he views the problem with optimism, as in another poem in *A Witness Tree* called "Our Hold on the Planet":

> Take nature altogether since time began,
> Including human nature, in peace and war,
> And it must be a little more in favour of man,
> Say a fraction of one per cent at the very least,
> Or our number living wouldn't be steadily more,
> Our hold on the planet wouldn't have so increased.

But one of the strangest and most powerful poems in *A Witness Tree* is "The Subverted Flower"; Jarrell has described it as "sinister, condemning, tender, . . . a flawed but extraordinary poem that at once embodies and states in almost abstract form his knowledge about part of love." This poem is quite unlike anything else Frost has written; it is as if the dark side of his vision was for once released completely, while the taut, nervous movement of the short lines seems to be the only thing that controls this vision at all. It is, perhaps, one of the most revealing of Frost's poems—not a conventionally personal poem, though, so much as a sudden, dramatic, naked glimpse into the man's inner struggles with his own instincts, emotions and thoughts:

> She drew back; he was calm:
> "It is this that had the power."
> And he lashed his open palm
> With the tender-hearted flower.
>
> She had to lean away.
> She dared not stir a foot,
> Lest movement should provoke
> The demon of pursuit
> That slumbers in a brute.
>
> A girl could only see
> That a flower had marred a man,
> But what she could not see
> Was that the flower might be
> Other than base or fetid:
> That the flower had done but part,
> And what the flower began
> Her own too meagre heart
> Had terribly completed.

This dark fairy story, this curious myth with its emphasis on perversity, makes a strange contrast with Frost's lucid and tender sonnets, poems which concentrate completely on the beauty of the woman loved. I know of few poems in English which are comparable, so far as feeling and plot go, with "The Subverted Flower." Coleridge's "Chrystabel" might usefully be compared with it, but that is a much longer poem and also one in which the poet himself does not seem so closely involved with the subject-matter of his poem.

A Witness Tree is one of Frost's most rewarding books. Published in 1942, it is one of the last of his volumes to be devoted solely to lyric verse. It contains love poems, descriptive poems, reflective poems, humorous verse. Whatever the mood or the subject, however, each poem is unmistakably the work of Robert Frost. The tone of voice, the detachment, the sudden confidence, the wry tenderness—all these qualities are Frost's, and the combination of them makes up what we instantly recognise as his poetic style. And the stars are, in this book, as important a part of his world picture as in any of the earlier collections:

> But no, I was out for stars:
> I would not come in.
> I meant not even if asked,
> And I hadn't been.

REFERENCES

1. *C.P.*, p. 271.
2. *C.P.*, p. 301.
3. *P.A.*, p. 43.

4. *C.P.*, p. 361.
5. *O.B.A.V.*, p. xxx.
6. *P.A.*, p. 69.

CHAPTER IV

STEEPLE BUSH, AN AFTERWORD, A MASQUE OF REASON, A MASQUE OF MERCY

The next book which Frost published was *A Masque of Reason*, but as it seems more useful to consider this together with *A Masque of Mercy*, I shall deal now with his last book of lyric poetry, *Steeple Bush*,[1] (and its companion, *An Afterword*) which was published in 1947. This volume includes an extremely condensed poem called "Directive." The poem is a warning, an instruction, an injunction; yet it lies beyond didacticism, largely because one feels the poet is learning about himself at least as much as he is instructing the reader. The poem is a kind of discovery, as well as an invitation:

> Back out of all this now too much for us,
> Back in a time made simple by the loss
> Of detail, burned, dissolved, and broken off
> Like graveyard marble sculpture in the weather,
> There is a house that is no more a house
> Upon a farm that is no more a farm
> And in a town that is no more a town.
> The road there, if you'll let a guide direct you
> Who only has at heart your getting lost,
> May seem as if it should have been a quarry. . . .
>
> I have kept hidden in the instep arch
> Of an old cedar at the waterside
> A broken drinking goblet like the Grail
> Under a spell so the wrong ones can't find it,

So can't get saved, as Saint Mark says they mustn't.
(I stole the goblet from the children's playhouse.)
Here are your waters and your watering-place.
Drink and be whole again beyond confusion.

This mysterious poem, half-elegy, half-parable, bears
some resemblance to an even more mysterious poem by
Robert Graves, "Instructions to the Orphic Adept":

You shall drink deep of that refreshing draught,
To become lords of the uninitiated
Twittering ghosts, Hell's countless populace—
To become heroes, knights upon swift horses,
Pronouncing oracles from tall white tombs
By the nymphs tended. They with honey water
Shall pour libations to you serpent shapes,
That you may drink.

Both these poems are personal yet minatory; each poet is
using his experience, not simply his knowledge, to instruct
and help others.

A poem which, unlike "Directive," works more by
statement than suggestion, is "Too Anxious For Rivers."
Of this poem, Lawrance Thompson[2] has written,

... "Too Anxious For Rivers" is related to Frost's
most revealing poetic statement of continuity [this is
one of the poet's abiding themes]: *West-Running Brook*.
There he explicitly invokes images drawn from
Lucretius and would seem to blend them with Herac-
litan metaphors such as these: the death of the earth
gives life to fire, the death of fire gives life to air, the
death of air gives life to water, and the death of water
gives life to earth, thus figuratively suggesting the end-
less cycle of birth and death and rebirth and continuity,
in nature. ... In his poem entitled "Too Anxious For
Rivers", the basic arrangement of imagery represents
a landscape vista where a stream flowing through
the foreground would seem to be blocked off by a

mountain in the background. . . . Taken symbolically
or (in this extremely puritanical poem) taken allegorically, the river is life, the mountain is death, the sea
is the life-beyond-death, and the rebuked questioner
implicitly may be any descendant of Adam who has a
tendency to ask too many questions about life and
death. . . . The poem develops . . . in such a way as
to mock the attempts of both science and religion to
explain first causes and last effects.

"Too Anxious For Rivers" is less puritanical and not
quite so explicit in matters of detail as Thompson suggests. His analysis of the poem is, in general, true, but
Frost is really much less didactic here than the critic has
tried to indicate. The poem grows by accumulation, by
the interweaving of statement with question; and though
it has a reflective and philosophical air, it also has something of the feeling of a story. In fact, Frost, even when he
is being abstract and metaphysical, often appears to be
telling a story. A narrative or a history is never very far
away. This tendency can be seen very clearly in a passage
from the middle of "Too Anxious For Rivers":

> The world as we know is an elephant's howdah;
> The elephant stands on the back of a turtle;
> The turtle in turn on a rock in the ocean.
> And how much longer a story has science
> Before she must put out the light on the children
> And tell them the rest of the story is dreaming?
> "You children may dream it and tell it tomorrow."

Steeple Bush lacks the unity of *A Witness Tree*. The
reason for this is partly that Frost seems a little at odds
with himself in the later book, and partly that many of
the poems are fragmentary, even if the fragments themselves are often very fine. The moods of the book range
from the slightly ironic wit of "To an Ancient":

> Your claims to immortality were two.
> The one you made, the other one you grew.
> Sorry to have no name for you but You.

to the childlike simplicity of "A Steeple on the House":

> What if it should turn out eternity
> Was but the steeple on our house of life
> That made our house of life a house of worship?

The power and effectiveness of this poem lie both in the tentativeness of its statement, and also in the absolute concreteness of the writing ("A spire and belfry coming on the roof | Means that a soul is coming on the flesh."). There is no ratiocination, simply an impulse that has been allowed to clothe itself in a series of extremely homely images. The cumulative effect is very remarkable. In a poem like "Sceptic," Frost would seem to be demonstrating that he lays no claim to any specific set of dogmas, but lives by one provisional belief after another. In "Sceptic," there is no elation, only pain:

> The universe may or may not be very immense.
> As a matter of fact there are times when I am apt
> To feel it close in tight against my sense
> Like a caul in which I was born and still am wrapped.

It is very hard to separate Frost's moods from his beliefs and this, probably, is what has so incensed Yvor Winters. It is worth quoting the whole of "Etherealizing," also in *Steeple Bush*, to show Frost's own attitude to this matter. If we read him carefully, we often find that he has, within his poems, answered most of the strictures of the critics:

> A theory if you hold it hard enough
> And long enough gets rated as a creed:
> Such as that flesh is something we can slough
> So that the mind can be entirely freed . . .
> Then when the arms and legs have atrophied,

And brain is all that's left of mortal stuff,
We can lie on the beach with the seaweed
And take our daily tide baths smooth and rough.
There once we lay as blobs of jellyfish
At evolution's opposite extreme.
But now as blobs of brain we'll lie and dream,
With only one vestigial creature wish:
Oh, may the tide be soon enough at high
To keep our abstract verse from being dry.

Frost, in his "abstract verse," has an almost unique
ability to simplify the universe to its most basic principles
—a cell, a star, a struggling creature on a beach—and
then to build up a system or a world from that. But the
world for him is not always the same, immutable one; it
changes from poem to poem. The excitement which even
his very few truly abstract poems generate is caused by
the poet's refusal to be satisfied or smug. No-one could be
further from complacency than Frost; and, on the other
hand, no-one could be further from unthinking and fruitless "spiritual drifting." As Jarrell has noted, his "obsessive themes" are "those of isolation, of extinction, and of
the final limitations of man."

In *Steeple Bush*, there are several poems in which Frost
mocks, fairly gently, at science; "Why Wait For Science"
is an example of this sort of literary squib:

Why wait for Science to supply the how
When any amateur can tell it now?

This poem, however, expresses a mood rather than a
settled attitude of mind. It is not so much science itself
which Frost castigates as the omniscience which some
scientists claim for themselves. And, what is more, it is
not simply scientific omniscience but *all* claims to omniscience that Frost distrusts.

An Afterword,[3] a sort of coda to *Steeple Bush*, contains
three poems—"Choose Something Like a Star," "From

Plane to Plane," a long narrative-reflective poem, and the very beautiful "Closed For Good." This last is a kind of farewell poem, a tribute by Frost to all his ancestors, both literary and otherwise:

> Much as I own I owe
> The passers of the past
> Because their to and fro
> Has cut this road to last,
> I owe them more today
> Because they've gone away.
>
> How often is the case
> I thus pay men a debt
> For having left a place
> And still do not forget
> To pay them some sweet share
> For having once been there.

This is the direct, economical, almost terse Frost, the poet of the love sonnets and of "Desert Places." "From Plane to Plane" is a very different kind of poem; it is a sort of conversation piece between two hired men, a country-man and a man from college. As is his custom in this type of poem, Frost employs blank verse, and it is amazing how flexible he makes this medium seen. It can carry equally effectively the colloquial

> They were giving corn
> A final going over with the hoe. . . .

and the allusively humorous

> "So I have heard and do in part believe it,"
> Dick said to old Pike, innocent of Shakespeare.

and the reflective

> "I like to think the sun's like you in that—
> Since you bring up the subject of the sun.
> This would be my interpretation of him.

He bestows summer on us and escapes
Before our realizing what we have
To thank him for. He doesn't want our thanks.
He likes to turn his back on gratitude
And avoid being worshipped as a god.
Our worship was a thing he had too much of
In the old days in Persia and Peru."

That last line reminds us that Frost is far from being an unlearned man. If he sometimes chooses to appear as the simple countryman who knows little of books, this is because he likes at times to hide his real self behind this mask or *persona*. Why does he do this? Why is he, sometimes, so evasive? It is not easy to answer such questions satisfactorily. Like most poets, and particularly lyric poets (writers who put so much of themselves and their lives, transmuted, into their work), Frost is extraordinarily sensitive to the discrepancy between his poetry and his life as it appears superficially to other men and women. To hide this shyness and diffidence, he sometimes poses (this word is not being used pejoratively) as a homespun philosopher, an unlearned farmer, and he does this not because he wants to deceive either himself or other people, but rather because he wants to diminish the gulf between the ease and simplicity of much of his work and the darkness and self-questioning of his own inner life. For lyric poets are peculiarly vulnerable to the sort of questioner who asks, "Why aren't you more like your poems?", "Did this really happen to you?", "Don't you feel embarrassed when people read such personal poems?" We have seen already, in *The Paris Review* interview, how Frost evades this kind of probing. In the Introduction to his *Complete Poems*, he has some revealing things to say both about his own work and about poetry in general:

For me the initial delight is the surprise of remembering something I didn't know I knew.... Political freedom is nothing to me. I bestow it right and left. All I would keep for myself is the freedom of my material—the condition of body and mind now and then to summons aptly from the vast chaos of all I have lived through. Scholars and artists thrown together are often annoyed at the puzzle of where they differ. Both work from knowledge; but I suspect they differ most importantly in the way their knowledge is come by. Scholars get theirs with conscientious thoroughness along projected lines of logic; poets theirs cavalierly and as it happens in and out of books. They stick to nothing deliberately, but let what will stick to them like burrs where they walk in the fields. . . . A poem may be worked over once it is in being but may not be worried into being.

From these remarks, it is easy to see that Frost prizes spontaneity above almost every other quality: but it is too often forgotten how much stress he also lays on discipline, patience, and watchfulness. Frost may say that a poem "begins in delight and ends in wisdom," but he never forgets the pain, care, and craftsmanship which temper the delight and help to achieve the wisdom.

A Masque of Reason[4] was published in 1945, a year before *Steeple Bush* and *A Masque of Mercy* appeared. The two masques make an illuminating comparison. *A Masque of Reason* is a short play which brings the Biblical story of Job up to date. The aim of the play is to justify God's ways to men; Frost's way of doing this is very different from that of Milton in *Paradise Lost*. Frost's play lacks the power and majesty of Milton's epic; one of the chief reasons for this is that the God of *A Masque of Reason* is too weak and too anthropomorphic. He explains his apparent injustice to men in the following ways, none of which carry much conviction:

> I've had you [Job] on my mind a thousand years
> To thank you some day for the way you helped me

> Establish once for all the principle
> There's no connection man can reason out
> Between his just deserts and what he gets.
>
> You would have supposed
> One who in the beginning *was* the Word
> Would be in a position to command it.
> I have to wait for words like anyone.
>
> Too long I've owed you this apology
> For the apparently unmeaning sorrow
> You were afflicted with in those old days.
> But it was of the essence of the trial
> You shouldn't understand it at the time.
> It had to seem unmeaning to have meaning.

From these lines, one can see how Yvor Winters was able
to make out a case for Frost's enthronement of unreason.
Indeed, God goes on to declare,

> your husband Job and I together
> Found out the discipline man needs most
> Was to learn his submission to unreason.

Yet this over-simplicist view is somewhat modified by
Job himself when he explains to God,

> Reason is, I suppose, the steering gear.
>
> Because I let You off
> From telling me Your reason, don't assume
> I thought you had none. Somewhere back
> I knew you had one.
>
> It seems to me
> An afterthought, a long, long afterthought.

To this, God replies, showing himself to be only too
humanly fallible,

Job, you must understand my provocation.
The tempter comes to me and I am tempted.
I'd had about enough of this derision
Of what I valued most in human nature.

God, then, seems to have little more power than
Satan. The universe as Frost sees it, at least in *A Masque of
Reason*, appears to be a stage on which God and Satan
wage continual war, and where neither is the victor for
long. From the Christian point of view, this is highly
unorthodox doctrine. God, in this masque, resembles
closely some of the opinionated countrymen in Frost's
narrative poems. He is humorous, argumentative, sometimes perverse. To Job, he says,

I was just showing off to the Devil. . . .

while of Satan, who makes a brief appearance, he
declares,

He's unhappy. Church neglect
And figurative use have pretty well
Reduced him to a shadow of himself.

To an orthodox Christian, *A Masque of Reason* does
seem rather unworthy of its vast subject. Frost's insistence
on slang and jocularity, his refusal to be wholly serious
for long, give his play a feeling of childishness. Yet
because Frost is a sophisticated, well-read man, the
childishness has none of the innocence or simplicity of the
English medieval miracle plays, which are, in part,
undoubtedly the model for his masques. This play's chief
failure is its embarrassing facetiousness; for example, we
quickly tire of Job's wife who dashes about trying to take
photographs of Job with God:

I want you in my group beside the throne—
Must have you. There, that's just the right arrange-
    ment.

Faced with God himself, Job's wife is neither awed nor abashed; she simply says,

> I'd know him by Blake's picture anywhere.

Lawrance Thompson[5] argues that Frost's emphasis in *A Masque of Reason* is "ultimately metaphysical and theistic" and that "Intimacy permits Job to ask his questions with all the ardor, boldness, even insolence of one participating in a family quarrel." To say these things seems both to rate the masque altogether too high and also to ignore the fact that the tone of the play is continually at odds with its arguments and message. In so carefully avoiding the solemn or portentous, Frost has fallen a victim to the opposite danger—that of superficiality. Briefly, by trying so hard not to be pretentious, he has only succeeded in making his play sound specious and frivolous. *A Masque of Reason* does seem, then, to be a failure; its brevity alone means that it gives the poet little space to lay out and present his arguments, let alone to resolve them. The masque also has another rather curious flaw. It is, in an odd way, literary; Job and God continually refer to Milton, Waller and Blake, either to reinforce their own arguments or to indicate where they themselves differ from these writers. Frost's intention in introducing Milton and the other poets was clearly to give his play a "timeless" quality. In fact, the references not only irritate the reader, but are also a constant reminder to him of time. The literary device defeats its own purpose because the reader finds himself continually asking precisely what period of time the masque is intended to cover.

A Masque of Reason is also disappointing because it reveals how shallow, for once, is Frost's conception both of the divine nature and of human nature. God, of course, is notoriously difficult to present in a play. Milton failed to convince us with his God the Father, and Frost fails too, though for very different reasons. But Frost has also failed with Job and his wife; the former seems to be merely a vehicle for argument, while the latter appears to represent little more than a laborious piece of comic interest. In other words, by bringing down the problem of evil and suffering to such very frivolous terms, Frost has not only not really answered any of the questions he poses, but he has not even presented his queries in a way that carries conviction. The second is a much more culpable weakness than the first, since *A Masque of Reason* is attempting to deal with a problem that has baffled men for centuries. But the unsatisfactory presentation of the problem is the poet's failure and no-one else's.

There is little doubt that a reader who had only seen *A Masque of Reason* would be inclined to assume that Frost was a poor arguer in verse, that he was unable to sustain any mood for long save the jocular or facetious one. Such a reader would be wrong, but he would be perfectly right in thinking that Frost has a very limited sense of the theatrical. He has, as we have seen, a powerful sense of drama, conflict and climax, but this sense is far more fully displayed in his lyrics and narrative poems than in either of his masques. The reason for this is probably that the characters in the two masques are little more than embodied ideas, while there is scarcely any action apart from the verbal action of the dialectic which continues in the course of the dialogue. Frost's attempts at wit, his "humorous" handling of Job's wife only contribute a little more unreality to the total effect.

A Masque of Reason appears, then, to be the only work of Frost's which may be said to deserve the fierce criticism which Yvor Winters[6] has made about the poet's general attitude towards thought and ideas. After praising Job's first speech for its "remarkable rhetoric," Winters goes on to make the following comments on the masque:

From that passage onward, through the references to

F

Blake and to the plywood throne, we have details which are offered merely for the shock of cleverness. ... Frost, the rustic realist of *North of Boston*, appears in his old age as a standard exemplar of irresponsible Romantic irony. ... The carefully flippant tone ... belongs to the tradition of Romantic irony ... and is used to make the ideas seem trivial [though this is surely not Frost's intention?]. The ideas and the tone together express the Romantic ennui or disillusionment which is born of spiritual laziness. ... There is no understanding of good and evil in themselves, of the metaphysical questions involved. Good is submission to an anthropomorphic and undignified God and is made to seem preposterous. ... If these concepts of good and evil were the only concepts available, or if they were the best concepts available, then Frost's satire would be justified. But they are not, and in reading the poem one can only be appalled at Frost's wilful ignorance, at his smug stupidity.

Most of these detailed judgments on the masque itself are just; Winters's criticism only becomes unfair and excessively harsh when he is talking about the man rather than the poems the man writes. Many of his literary strictures are also flawed (I am not only referring to his essay on Frost now) simply because he constantly refers to large concepts, such as good and evil, without attempting to establish either the foundations on which these concepts rest or the weight which he personally attaches to them. This is why Winters's general attacks on Frost are so often completely wide of the mark. On the other hand, his particular judgments are usually worth some consideration.

A Masque of Reason is one of Frost's very few complete failures. He is a prolific poet and he has written and succeeded with far more difficult tasks than this one. I have tried to indicate the nature of and reasons for his

failure, but it is not sufficient to view the weaknesses of
the masque merely as literary weaknesses. They also
indicate the limitations of trying to balance and maintain
too many opposites; this attitude is well suited to lyric
poetry, where mood, emotion and ideas run together,
and where one lyric may try out, as it were, a concept
which has previously been opposed or rejected in an
earlier poem. Provisional beliefs and judgments are
adequate for such poems because, in them, Frost is
always arguing with himself, meditating and then sharing
the fruits of his meditation with his readers. In didactic
and dramatic verse, however (and *A Masque of Reason* is
an attempt at both *genres*) Frost seems to be hiding his
own seriousness behind a front of jocularity and bluff-
ness. In other words, he seems to be deeply embarrassed
both by his characters and by the ideas which they are
putting forth. It is paradoxical that where he has most
opportunity to wear a mask, he is most clumsy, most
facetious, and, finally, most unacceptable. Frost is a
better poet and a more satisfactory thinker when he is
content with "walking naked."

A Masque of Mercy, a companion piece for *A Masque of
Reason*, is Frost's equivalent of Milton's *Paradise Regained*.
Unlike Milton, Frost is more successful with his handling
of the New Testament than he was with his Old Testament. One reason for this is that he wisely never introduces Christ into his play. His Old Testament God was
an almost total failure, and it does seem that when he
came to write his second masque Frost recognised that he
had little gift for portraying the transcendent and sublime
in the form of a character in a play.

A Masque of Mercy[7] is set in a New York bookstore and
its chief characters are Jonah, Keeper, Keeper's Wife,
Jesse Bel, and Paul (a modern version of St Paul). Jonah
appears in the shop and complains bitterly that he has
lost the power to prophesy. The central conflict of the play
is set forth in the lines which are put into Jonah's mouth:

I'm in the Bible, all done out in story.
I've lost my faith in God to carry out
The threats he makes against the city evil.
I can't trust God to be unmerciful.

The argument of *A Masque of Mercy* is far more subtle and
far more skilfully deployed than that of the earlier play.
There are a number of irritating plays on words, as in the
following lines,

JESSE BEL: He is our analyst.
JONAH: Your analyst?
KEEPER: Who keeps our bookstore annals.

but in general Frost maintains the seriousness of his
theme and only breaks it with humour when the tension
is becoming too great. And this, perhaps, is the most
interesting fact about the masque: it really does engender
and communicate a sense of urgency; the arguments are
humanly important arguments, not simply dispassiona-
ately presented fragments of dialectic. The reader really
cares about the characters, particularly about Paul and
Jonah. As Lawrance Thompson[8] has indicated, ". . .
while the heretical flavor or tone of the handling is quite
obvious, the action eventually resolves into notions
congenial to a fairly conventional viewpoint." He goes
on:

the dominant thematic concern of *A Masque of Mercy*
may be said to pivot once again on the limitations of
human knowledge as it involves different responses to
different kinds of fear, starting with the wisdom-
unwisdom of man's fearing God.

Because Frost is not content with mere abstractions in
A Masque of Mercy, because the whole argument and plot
of the play are presented in terms of human passion, this
second masque carries far more conviction, and involves
the reader far more closely, than the first one. The verbal
excitement of the dialogue is quickly immersed in

emotion; it is never divorced from the demands of the characters. As in *A Masque of Reason*, all the action is in the speeches, but where the first masque was either facetious or else over-cerebral, the second is compassionate, serious and committed.

The success of *A Masque of Mercy* is due largely to something we have already become familiar with in Frost's best lyrics and narrative-reflective poems—namely, the glittering compression and complexity of the arguments, the dexterous play of ideas, the neat, yet not superficial, opposing of one way of thought with another. Yet Frost is by no means committed to ambiguity for its own sake; he lays one set of notions alongside another in order to reveal the relevance or appropriateness of each. Thus Paul says to Jonah, in a crucial speech:

> You are the universal fugitive,
> Escapist as we say, though you are not
> Running away from Him you think you are
> But from his mercy-justice contradiction.
> Mercy and justice are a contradiction.
> But here's where your evasion has an end.
> I have to tell you something that will spoil
> Indulgence in your form of melancholy
> Once and for all. I'm going to make you see
> How relatively little justice matters.

As impulse claims precedence over logic in *A Masque of Reason*, so mercy, working through apparent unreasonableness, triumphs over mere justice in *A Masque of Mercy*. In these two masques, whatever their aesthetic value may be, we are able to perceive two of Frost's lifelong conflicts being worked out. It is significant, surely, that he is more successful in proving the supremacy of mercy than he is in enthroning unreason.

A Masque of Mercy also contains many of Frost's minor and incidental obsessions. His dislike of adamant orthodoxy is everywhere apparent, and even some of his

slightly eccentric preoccupations are given some sort of
consideration. His minor obsessions pale before the sureness and conviction in the following speech; it is spoken
by Paul:

> Christ came to introduce a break with logic
> That made all other outrage seem as child's play:
> The Mercy on the Sin against the Sermon.
> Strange no one ever thought of it before Him.
> 'Twas lovely and its origin was love.

And the heart of the masque is revealed in these words
spoken by Keeper:

> An irresistible impossibility.
> A lofty beauty no one can look up to.

Later in the play, Keeper is given a long speech which
seems to contain most of Frost's own inner convictions.
The poet appears to be deeply involved here:

> If even the face of man's too bright a light
> To look at long directly (like the sun),
> Then how much more the face of truth must be.
> We were not given eyes or intellect
> For all the light at once the source of light—
> For wisdom that can have no counter-wisdom.
> In our subscription to the sentiment
> Of one God we provide He shall be one
> Who can be many Gods to many men,
> His church on earth a Roman Pantheon;
> Which is our greatest hope of rest from war.
> Live and let live, believe and let believe.
> 'Twas said the lesser gods were only traits
> Of the one awful God. Just so the saints
> Are God's white light refracted into colours.

Keeper and Paul share between them most of Frost's
own findings and beliefs. When Jonah dies at the end of
the masque, they each have important points to make and
conclusions to draw. Paul declares:

> We have to stay afraid deep in our souls
> Our sacrifice, the best we have to offer,
> And not our worst nor secondbest, our best,
> Our very best, our lives laid down like Jonah's,
> Our lives laid down in war and peace, may not
> Be found acceptable in Heaven's sight.
> And that they may be is the only prayer
> Worth praying. May my sacrifice
> Be found acceptable in Heaven's sight.

Keeper's final speech is only partially conclusive; there is nothing tricked or facile about it:

> My failure is no different from Jonah's.
> We both have lacked the courage in the heart
> To overcome the fear within the soul
> And go ahead to any accomplishment.
> Courage is what it takes and takes the more of
> Because the deeper fear is so eternal. . . .
>
> Nothing can make injustice just but mercy.

The verse in *A Masque of Mercy* is more subtle, varied and flexible than in the earlier play. The intellectual disputes are closely knitted into the texture of the iambic pentameters. Throughout this play, in fact, one feels that Frost is more at ease, and also more involved than he was in *A Masque of Reason*. His passion for contraries is very obvious, but the facetiousness and perversity which inform the first play are less in evidence in the second.

There is no doubt, however, that in his discussions on religion, Frost shows a marked tendency to have it both ways. Thus in *A Masque of Reason*, he wants to enthrone impulse at the expense of logic, even though he uses logic to convince us that the enthronement is necessary. Similarly, his arguments for mercy in the second masque spring from an inner conviction (or so it often appears in the context) that there is still a great deal to be said for the Old Testament conception of justice. Yet *A Masque of*

Mercy succeeds where *A Masque of Reason* fails largely because the second play is far more impassioned and emotional; Frost's very failure to argue coolly has been responsible for the overall success of the masque. Paul, Jonah and Keeper are characters, not ciphers.

A Masque of Mercy does have its weak moments, however. Occasionally it is self-consciously literary, as when Paul quotes Francis Thompson's "I fled him down the nights and down the days; I fled him, down the arches of the years." But such lapses are far less frequent in this play than they were in the first. Frost presumably introduces the names of poets and quotations from their work in order to give resonance and confirmation to his own verse arguments; usually such interpolations only succeed in reminding the reader of the artificial conventions of the masque itself. They thus weaken the general effect, they do not strengthen its impact.

Perhaps *A Masque of Mercy* is more deeply felt and carries greater conviction simply because it is so much concerned with fear—an emotion which appears in different forms throughout Frost's work. Fear is the one thing about which this poet is never ambivalent. He sees it both as a dominant human feeling and also as one of the chief factors governing the universe; there is nothing theoretical about it. Maybe the relationship between darkness and light produces the tension which we sense in all Frost's best poems, even the most superficially tranquil ones. The darkness is felt, even if only by its absence. Sometimes Frost confronts it with stoicism, sometimes with humour, sometimes with a barely restrained terror. But he is never hysterical, and the horror he sees "deep down things" is the more convincing because he never gets indignant or excited about it. He accepts, not because he likes this condition of things, but because he understands its necessity. And since he faces pain and darkness with absolute honesty, Frost also feels free to be completely joyful and happy in his tender love poems, in the lyrics which show his delight in nature, and in the narrative poems which manifest his pleasure in the ordinariness and eccentricities of men and women.

Frost's "wisdom" is thus seen to be a much more complicated matter than a mere handful of aphorisms spoken by a "simple countryman." Randall Jarrell[9] remarks about Frost's attitude towards life:

> This recognition of the essential limitations of man, without denial or protest or rhetoric or palliation, is very rare and very valuable, and rather usual in Frost's best poetry. One is reminded of Empson's thoughtful and truthful comment on Gray's "Elegy": "Many people, without being communists, have been irritated by the complacence in the massive calm of the poem. . . . And yet what is said is one of the permanent truths; it is only in degree that any improvement of society would prevent wastage of human powers; the waste even in a fortunate life, the isolation even of a life rich in intimacy, cannot but be felt deeply, and is the central feeling of tragedy."

Frost's acceptance of things as they are does not prevent him from possessing and communicating the tragic sense. His juggling with opposites, his play among contraries—this activity is not a smug way of trying to impose order where there is no obvious order; rather it is an acknowledgment of wholeness, an admission that pain, evil and guilt are as real as pleasure, goodness and suffering. For, above all else, Frost's view of life is a complete one; it finds room for everything, even if it cannot explain everything. And, what is more, Frost is willing to admit that there are many things which he cannot explain. He has neither the Romantic poet's readiness to exclude all that does not fit into a sense of the transitoriness of things, nor the sceptic's refusal even to attempt to answer the questions which all men, who think or feel at all, are faced with at some time in their lives. In his best lyrics, Frost shows that his zest for life is tempered, but not minimised, by his sense of tragedy; he also shows that a strong feeling for the physical presence and concreteness of things is not incompatible with a certain hankering after abstractions. Physical objects and spiritual matters are opposites, and it is the aim of Frost's poetry to record both their interplay and their antagonism.

REFERENCES

1. *C.P.*, p. 407.
2. *Rt. Ft.*, p. 26.
3. *C.P.*, p. 437.
4. *C.P.*, p. 447.
5. *Rt. Ft.*, p. 30.

6. *O.M.P.*, p. 191.
7. *C.P.*, p. 467.
8. *Rt. Ft.*, p. 34.
9. *P.A.*, p. 48.

CHAPTER V

THE INFLUENCE AND PHILOSOPHY
OF FROST

Since the nineteenth century, American poetry has developed in two main streams; the first began with the free, pulsating, incantatory verse of Walt Whitman, while the second started with the experiments and innovations of Pound and Eliot. Frost owes a little to both traditions, though he has, on the whole, tended to work from and continue an earlier tradition and thus, finally, create a tradition of his own. His first poems were somewhat Georgian in flavour and only when he returned to the United States to spend the rest of his life there did his work acquire that tang, flavour, tone and accent which are unmistakably American. This flavour and tone have seeped into his style and idiom and appear not simply in the form of slang or colloquialisms but as a decided part of a complete language. Reading Frost, one never forgets that he is, above all else, an *American* poet. This is shown in "The Witch of Coös":

> Folks think a witch who has familiar spirits
> She could call up to pass a winter evening,
> But won't, should be burned at the stake or something.

in "For Once, Then, Something":

> What was that whiteness?
> Truth? A pebble of quartz? For once, then something.

in this extract from "A Hillside Thaw":

> It takes the moon for this. The sun's a wizard
> By all I tell; but so's the moon a witch.

and in these lines from "A Servant to Servants":

> The worst that you can do
> It set me back a little more behind.
> I shan't catch up in this world anyway.
> I'd *rather* you'd not go unless you must.

If the first important influences on Frost were English ones, he is remarkably free from any other European traditions or innovations. His work is entirely lacking in that air of cosmopolitanism, that ease among French and Italian styles and models, that we find, in different ways, in Eliot, Pound and Wallace Stevens. In this, but in no other way, Frost resembles Whitman; stylistically, of course, he is far removed from that poet.

Wallace Stevens also makes an interesting comparison with Frost. Stevens's exotic objects—his pictures, still lives, vases, and so on—seldom appear in his poems for their own sake; on the contrary, they are generally merely opportunities for aesthetic inquiries. Frost's country scenes, however, his farming, animals, seasons, men and women, are acknowledged and admitted into his verse because they are interesting and valuable in themselves. They often prompt philosophical reflection, it is true, but one seldom feels that that is their whole *raison d'être*.

In one respect, however, Frost and Stevens do resemble each other. Each has a highly developed sense of form. Stevens was always much more willing to make experiments, though Frost, even when he uses the most conventional and familiar forms and cadences, often brings new life to what had become dull and hackneyed.

Frost's feeling for form is as strong as John Peale Bishop's, John Crowe Ransom's or Allen Tate's. And it is this which has had the strongest influence on the younger American poets. Richard Wilbur, Edgar Bowers, Donald Hall and Adrienne Rich all reveal this influence in their own poetry. Sometimes the effect of Frost is more than simply a formal one. The following lines from a poem by

Adrienne Rich, "Autumn Equinox", show that she has been influenced by Frost in the matter of subject-matter as well as that of style:

> So Lyman came to ask me of my father:
> Stiff-collared, shy, not quite the man I'd dreamed—
> (Byron and Matthew Arnold vaguely mingled
> Without the disadvantages of either.)

The parenthesis here, the sly reference to dead poets, the terse, colloquial tone of voice—all these things bring Frost quickly to the reader's mind.

Donald Hall, on the other hand, in a few light squibs which are given the overall title, "Conduct and Work," reminds us of Frost in his humorous mood. Here is one of Hall's verse epigrams:

> The rot that eats the poem up
> Comes from the face I learned at school,
> When over every friendly cup
> I smiled to suffer any fool.

Frost has probably had a more far-reaching, though much less perceptible, effect on the younger American poets than either Pound or Eliot. There is something calm and steadfast about his work which inspires confidence. He is also unmistakably American; his poems are never exotic or eclectic. If a feeling for the land of America is expressed with more reticence in Frost's work than it is in Whitman's, this very reticence and refusal to be rhetorical make a strong appeal to a more self-conscious generation than Whitman's.

In England, Frost has scarcely ever been a direct influence. Auden's juvenile poems (particularly those uncollected ones which Christopher Isherwood has reprinted in his own *Lions and Shadows*) contain echoes of his voice, but only on C. Day Lewis, now a middle-aged poet, can his work be said to have had a marked effect. Indeed, in the section entitled "Florence: Works of Art"

in Day Lewis's *Italian Visit*, there is a rather clever parody
of Frost. It begins:

> There was never a morning quite so tremendous again.
> The birth, you think? I'm not for setting great store
> By birth. Births are beginnings. And anyway
> She only wanted to sleep off the pain
> Which had made her a beast among beasts on the
>   cow-house floor.
> Shepherds and magnates tiptoeing through the hay
> (You get all kinds at an inn, she drowsily thought),
> Even the babe—they were part of a snowdrift trance,
> Almost unreal.

Like most lyric poets, Frost has had, on the whole, a
fugitive influence on other writers. His ideas are often too
idiosyncratic and too involved with his own personal
feelings to have had a direct influence on younger poets.
His style and his tone of voice, while they have certainly
influenced other writers in the direction of clarity and
simplicity, are too fully developed, too completely
realised in Frost's own work to have had an all-pervading
effect on anyone else. For the truth is that it is the great
flawed or incomplete poets—the Pounds rather than the
Eliots—who tend to be of most use to the poets who follow them. There is something formidable about a writer
whose technique and craftsmanship are as nearly perfect
as Frost's. We admire but we cannot imitate, at least not
for long or to much purpose. The influence Frost exerts
does not arise from particular poems so much as from
what the poet himself represents as a man.

Frost's poetry has, then, had a general and overall
influence rather than a specific one. Perhaps a parallel to
it can be found in England in the poetry of Robert
Graves. Like Frost, Graves is a master of form, a highly
skilled craftsman, and an idiosyncratic thinker. On the
younger English poets, he has had a similar influence
to that of Frost on contemporary poets in America.

Simplicity, honesty, directness, and clarity—these are the qualities which Graves has always fostered in his work, and it is these qualities that we tend to find in the best English poets of the present time. Like Frost again, Graves is a somewhat isolated figure, an intensely English poet (as Frost is an intensely American one) who has played little or no part in the literary movements or experiments of the past half-century. Both poets regard the writing of poetry as the most important activity of their lives; both show an almost religious reverence for it. In one important respect, however, they do differ. Graves has an almost fanatical dislike for the long poem and for the poem of ideas, while Frost has no such suspicion or limitation. Graves has deliberately restricted the function of poetry, where Frost has always sought to use all the potentialities of the art. In this, Frost is a far more important poet than Graves; and in range, scope, profundity and achievement, he is greatly superior to the English poet.

To American and English readers, as opposed to writers and practitioners, of poetry, Frost is almost a living classic. "Stopping By Woods on a Snowy Evening," with its haunting conclusion:

> But I have promises to keep,
> And miles to go before I sleep,
> And miles to go before I sleep.

is as familiar to American schoolchildren as Tennyson's "Break, Break, Break" and Wordsworth's "Daffodils" are in Britain. Subtle and complex as Frost's poems often are, they have a surface simplicity and lucidity which make them admirable introductions to the study of poetry. A child would appreciate and indeed understand him when he would find Stevens, Pound, Eliot, and even Auden obscure and impenetrable. It is not, therefore, surprising that the feeling of Frost, his tone of voice, have seeped into the early poems of some of the finest young

American poets. We have seen already how reluctant Frost is to give his opinions, and how elusive he often is when asked how he writes his poems. In the interview which he gave to *The Paris Review*[1] in 1960, he did, nevertheless, make some interesting remarks about the influence of other poets on his own work. When asked why he went to live in Gloucestershire before the First World War, Frost replied,

> My choice was almost unconscious in those days. I didn't know whether I had any position in the world at all, and I wasn't choosing positions. You see, my instinct was not to belong to any gang, and my instinct was against being confused with the—what do you call them?—they called themselves Georgians, Edwardians, something like that, the people Edward Marsh was interested in. Yes, I knew Hulme, knew him quite well, but I never went to one of those meetings. I said to Pound, "What do you do?" He said, "Rewrite each other's poems." And I said, "Why?" He said, "To squeeze the water out of them." "That sounds like a parlor game to me," I said. "And I'm a serious artist."—kidding, you know. And he laughed and he didn't invite me any more.

Speaking of Wallace Stevens, Frost said, in the same interview, "Once he said to me, 'You write on subjects.' And I said, 'You write on bric à brac.' . . . No, I had no affinity with him. We were friends." Frost has always been reluctant to admit any obvious influences on his poetry. To a comment made by Lionel Trilling about the "darkness" and "terror" in some of his poems, he said

> . . . when he began comparing me to Sophocles and D. H. Lawrence I was completely at sea. What the two of them had to do with me, you know. Might be I might like it about Sophocles, but I'd be puzzled, oh, utterly at sea about D. H. Lawrence.

Frost's reluctance to admit or at least to speak about the poets who have influenced him is just one more example of his strong need to protect himself and his work from intrusion. The facetiousness which he occasionally displays in *The Paris Review* interview is another aspect of the same thing. Frost always wishes to communicate by means of his verse, certainly, but he has a deep distrust of anything which suggests an analysis of his talent. He does not want to explore the sources of his poetic gift. He is an extremely thoughtful and meditative man, but the nature of his poetic insight is probably the only thing he never probes or questions. Its existence is enough for him; to attempt to take it to pieces would seem to Frost both a dangerous and an impertinent activity. It is significant that scarcely any of his poems have, as their chief subject-matter, the making of poems—a subject which has been exploited only too often by many other poets during the last twenty-five years. "Closed for Good" is almost the only poem of Frost's which is directly concerned with his art and talent, and even this poem is more concerned with the poets who preceded Frost than with his own poetry or his attitude to it.

In 1957, Frost contributed a short Introduction to the paperback anthology, *The New Poets of England and America*, edited by Donald Hall, Robert Pack and Louis Simpson. In this Introduction, he had some advice to give young poets which throws a good deal of light on his own attitude to development, influence and poetic maturity:

Poetry has been a great concern of school all down the ages. A large part of reading in school always has been and still is poetry; and it is but an extension from the metaphors of poetry out into all thinking, scientific and philosophic. In fact the poet and scholar have so much in common and live together so naturally that it is easy to make too much of a mystery about where they part company. . . . The poet's instinct is to shun

G

or shed more knowledge than he can sing or swing.
His most available knowledge is acquired uncon-
sciously. Something warns him dogged determination
however profound can only end in doggerel... all
poets I have ever heard of struck their note long before
forty, the deadline for contributions to this book. The
statistics are all in favour of their being as good and
lyric as they will ever be.... Maturity will come.
We mature.

Frost is a far more complex writer than is often sup-
posed; he is complicated and also full of contradictions.
He is a highly-conscious artist who is constantly lauding
impulse, a penetrating thinker who is afraid of being
discovered in the act of thought, a countryman who conceals behind his feeling for the land a sophisticated
attitude towards men and their motives. Before we
examine the actual content of Frost's thought in more
detail, it may be useful to inquire just why he feels the
need to wear masks and to assume so many *personae*. One
of the chief reasons is surely that Frost, though he would
certainly hate such a thing to be said, is profoundly
aware of the dilemmas which seem to be part of the
American writer's inheritance. But where other writers,
such as James or Eliot, have recognised and tried to
accept their predicament, Frost has tried, as far as possible, to ignore even the existence of his. Yet his life has
been as conventional as that of many other modern
American poets; he has been able to cultivate and live by
his writing simply because American universities are so
constituted that they have room for and welcome
creative writers. Frost's life as a farmer has never really
been his main life.

The early years as a poet which Frost led in England
have left him with traces of the curious attitude which
most English people adopt towards poets; they applaud
the amateur and distrust deeply anything which savours

of professionalism in poetry. In the United States, the
situation is totally different; the poet is a professional,
however unorthodox the nature of his profession may
seem. In Frost, this feeling for amateurism, combined
with a firm and profound dedication to his art, has
produced a slightly ambivalent attitude towards poetry in
general. As a result, Frost is not quite at ease with himself, and he sometimes hides this unease either behind
facetiousness or behind the pretence that his attitude
towards his work is a frivolous one. None of this shows in
his poetry except in *A Masque of Reason* and in a few verse
jokes and epigrams. But, on the other hand, the ambi-
valence is present in Frost's work on a deeper level than
that of self-consciousness or shyness. It appears in the
taste for contraries, in the opposition of worlds of light
with worlds of darkness, in the passion for balancing one
idea against its opposite, in the conflicts between good
and evil, reason and instinct, conflicts which Frost is
always reluctant to resolve completely. It is possible to
see, in fact, that Frost's whole personality is closely
connected with the philosophy which can be observed
evolving in the poetry itself. It is not that he only believes
what he wants to believe, but rather that the nature of
his own character has affected the emphasis which he
places on certain ideas and concepts.

It is not easy to set down Frost's central beliefs, partly
because they do not conform to any orthodox pattern and
partly because they are essentially provisional—notes by
the way rather than adamant and firmly-held dogmas.
Frost's beliefs are discovered in and through his poetry;
as with Wordsworth and with Yeats, his ideas have
grown up and developed with his verse. His faith or
philosophy is not something separate from his work but an
integral part of it. As Lawrance Thompson[2] has pointed
out, "His primary artistic achievement, which is an
enviable one, in spite of shortcomings, rests on his blend-
ing of thought and emotion and symbolic imagery within

the confines of the lyric." Perhaps the only other modern
poet writing in English who has not taken refuge in the
esoteric and whose beliefs are an essential part of his
verse is Edwin Muir: but where Muir worked through
allegory and all its implications, Frost's approach is
more realistic, more naturalistic even. Thus metaphor,
for him, does not have an autonomous life of its own. Its
validity depends on the world we all know and see.

Frost's philosophy is best understood if we remember
the arguments in favour of impulse in *A Masque of Reason*
and the argument for mercy in *A Masque of Mercy*. With
more complex matters, Frost has helped us by making an
interesting prose statement about his position (quoted by
Lawrance Thompson[3]):

> When in doubt, there is always form for us to go on
> with. Anyone who has achieved the least form to be
> sure of it, is lost to the larger excruciations. I think it
> must stroke faith the right way. The artist, the poet,
> might be expected to be more aware of such assurance.
> But it is really everybody's sanity to feel it and live by
> it. . . . The background is hugeness and confusion
> shading away from where we stand into black and utter
> chaos; and against the background any small man-
> made figure of order and concentration. What pleasanter
> than that it should be so. . . . To me, any little form
> I assert on it is velvet, as the saying is, and to be con-
> sidered for how much more it is than nothing. If I were a
> Platonist I should have to consider it, I suppose, for
> how much less it is than everything.

Throughout Frost's poems we are aware of this search
for and discovery of order; the sheer elegance of his
poetic performance is itself partly a defiant gesture
against chaos, and partly a triumphant assertion of order
through man's own ability to discover it in art. But fear
of chaos is also a dominant theme in Frost's work; an

early poem called "A Fear," in *North of Boston*, with its concluding lines:

> You understand that we have to be careful.
> This is a very, very lonely place.

expresses the same emotion as the later poem "Desert Places":

> I have it in me so much nearer home
> To scare myself with my own desert places.

But two later poems, in *Steeple Bush*, are more crucial to Frost's attitude towards fear because they attempt to analyse the emotion rather than simply to express it. Thus in the first poem, "The Fear of God," Frost declares:

> If you should rise from Nowhere up to Somewhere,
> From being No one up to being Some one,
> Be sure to keep repeating to your self
> You owe it to an arbitrary god
> Whose mercy to you rather than to others
> Won't bear too critical examination.

"The Fear of Man," which balances "The Fear of God," is much more reassuring and relaxed:

> But there are little street lights she should trust
> So jewel steady in the wind and dust.

What is most noticeable in all Frost's reflective poems is an almost total absence of despair or pessimism; it is not that he shuns darkness or difficulties—quite the reverse—but rather that something in his own mind and imagination makes him eager to accept, to examine, and sometimes to reconcile, opposites. He realises—to put the matter on a very simple level indeed—that without darkness there would be no light, without evil there would be no possibility of freely choosing good, without death, no life as we know it.

If there is no despair in Frost, neither is there any placidity or complacency. He accepts the condition of

man but this does not mean that he does not sometimes
rail against it. All this is well expressed in a sonnet, "The
Flood," from *West-Running Brook*:

> Blood has been harder to dam back than water.
> Just when we think we have it impounded safe
> Behind new barrier walls (and let it chafe!),
> It breaks away in some new kind of slaughter.
> We choose to say it is let loose by the devil;
> But power of blood itself releases blood.
> It goes by right of being such a flood
> Held high at so unnatural a level.
> It will have outlet, brave and not so brave.
> Weapons of war and implements of peace
> Are but the points at which it finds release.
> And now it is once more the tidal wave
> That when it has swept by leaves summits stained.
> Oh, blood will out. It cannot be contained.

In a short poem like this, Frost manages to convey far
more about his ideas, and his *feelings* about his ideas, than
in the long stretches of argument in, say, *A Masque of
Reason*. In his short poems, Frost's answers even to the
most abstract or metaphysical questions never feel theoretical; they are practical, concrete, down-to-earth. C.
Day Lewis[4] explains the reason for this when he says:

> ... no less than his preoccupation with hard fact, his
> language—cautious, dry, reticent, slow, ruminative—
> reveals the depths of his roots in the New England
> countryside, where for many years he farmed his own
> land. No working farmer is a romantic—not about
> Nature, at any rate. Mr. W. H. Auden has pointed out
> that Frost's poems on natural objects ... are always
> concerned with them not as foci for mystical medita-
> tion or starting-points for fantasy, but as things with
> which and on which man acts in the course of the daily
> work of gaining a livelihood.

This comment by Auden has been quoted already, but it seems worth repeating here because it has a particular relevance to any detailed examination of Frost's modes of thought.

It is, perhaps paradoxically, easier to examine Frost's attitude to rather vague concepts such as fate and free-will, than to be sure precisely what his beliefs about Christianity are. There is little doubt that he *is* a Christian, but there is also no doubt at all that his own faith scarcely conforms to any of the orthodoxies that most of us are familiar with. Frost, particularly in his early poems, often invokes God, and in his two masques we see that this God is a personal deity with whom man can enter into some sort of relationship. On the other hand, Frost's many poems about darkness, chaos, isolation and loneliness—Eliot's "vacant, interstellar spaces"—make it clear that God's presence in the universe often seems withdrawn or concealed. The poet does not deny His existence, but he is frequently very much occupied with describing or suggesting how it feels to live in a world bereft of God. This is just one more example of the duality, complexity and ambiguity of Frost's vision of life. He can never satisfy himself by presenting one side of a situation only, and this makes his view of life extraordinarily complete and reverberant. And further, where he cannot understand, Frost is always willing to say so. His integrity is far more deeply-rooted than his wit or occasional flashes of apparent irresponsibility.

It may be useful to give one or two random examples of the way in which Frost does at times introduce a deity. The first is taken from "A Prayer in Spring," a poem in *A Boy's Will*:

> For this is love and nothing else is love,
> The which it is reserved for God above
> To sanctify to what far ends he will,
> But which it only needs that we fulfil.

The next quotation comes from "Sitting By a Bush in Broad Daylight," which appears in *West-Running Brook*:

> God once declared he was true
> And then took the veil and withdrew,
> And remember how final a hush
> Then descended of old on the bush.

And in *A Further Range*, God is invoked at the end of a poem called "The Gold Hesperidee":

> God saw him dancing in the orchard path,
> But mercifully kept the passing crowd
> From witnessing the fault of one so proud.
> And so the story wasn't told in Gath;
> In gratitude for which Square Matthew vowed
> To walk a graver man restrained in wrath.

And, finally, here are some stanzas from "Astrometaphysical," in *Steeple Bush*:

> My love for every Heaven
> O'er which you, Lord, have lorded,
> From number One to Seven
> Should be rewarded.
>
> It may not give me hope
> That when I am translated
> My scalp will in the cope
> Be constellated.
>
> But if that seems to tend
> To my undue renown,
> At least it ought to send
> Me up, not down.

These quotations show how variable Frost's attitude to God and the idea of God is; he can move from the awed to the familiar, and from the frightened to the jocular with great ease. If his attitude to God is never the same for long, Frost, nonetheless, never seriously questions his existence or his power.

There is almost nothing of the mystic in Frost. He does not seek in nature either a sense of oneness with all created things or union with God. There is nothing Platonic in his view of life; everything is good and valuable in itself, not because it is a fore-shadowing of something else. When Frost says:

All revelation has been ours.

he means, literally and precisely, that. He is fairly taciturn about what happens to us after death, partly because he finds so much to engage his attention here and now. There are sufficient wonders, natural and supernatural, in everyday life as far as Frost is concerned; he is not, therefore, a visionary poet in the sense that Blake and Wordsworth were. He has no wish to prophesy. If at times he sounds didactic or hectoring, this is largely because Frost is as eager to instruct and convince himself as he is to do these things for other people.

Any purely intellectual examination of his personal philosophy is bound to falsify the poems a little. If we search in his poetry only for what Frost thinks and believes, we shall miss some of the most important things in them—the passion just held in check, the precision of observation, the tenderness and compassion, the occasional bewilderment. As Lawrance Thompson[5] has said:

... while much of Frost's poetry suggests that he cannot resist figurative utterances concerning his wavering yet centered spiritual preoccupations, we have at least seen that he often prefers to reveal-conceal some of his most intimate and personal beliefs through poetic indirections which grow more meaningful because they do contain and maintain elements of self-contradiction. ... Frost's central point of departure (or return) is a firmly rooted belief in both nature and human nature as at least poetically relatable within a design which has its ultimate source in a divine plan, a plan with which man collaborates to the best of his limited ability.

In spite of its entire lack of pretension, its modest and restrained tone, Frost's poetry invites the largest and most complex questions. Is poetry a communication, a kind of self-expression, a form of thought, or a way of life? These and many other queries enter the mind of the careful and conscientious reader of Frost's work. The reason for this is that the wholeness of his poetry, the assurance that is never far from humility, the exultation in language coupled with the sudden extraordinary silences, make the reader aware of the tremendous power of poetry, its strength and its ability to haunt. A man of fierce contradictions, Frost himself has always been reluctant to talk much about the sources and potentialities of poetry; he is far more reticent on this subject than he is when faced with large philosophical or religious questions. It will be of value, therefore, to attempt to put together some of the fragmentary remarks which he has made about his own attitude to the writing of verse. There can be no doubt that his feelings about this subject are an important part of his whole philosophy of life. Yet "art for art's sake" would have no meaning for Frost simply because he cannot envisage art as separate from the many other manifestations of life and man's awareness of life.

In the interview which he gave to Harvey Breit,[6] Frost made some revealing remarks about his position with regard to his own work:

One thing I care about . . . is taking poetry as the first form of understanding. Say it: my *favourite* form of understanding. If poetry isn't understanding all, the whole world, then it isn't worth anything. . . . Too many poets delude themselves by thinking the mind is dangerous and must be left out. Well, the mind is dangerous and must be left in.

This last remark should be a warning to critics who tend to think of Frost as a poet of immediate impulse only.

Frost continues:

If a writer were to say he planned a long poem dealing with Darwin and evolution, we would be tempted to say it's going to be terrible. And yet you remember Lucretius. He admired Epicurus as I admired, let's say, Darwin. And he wrote a great poem. It's in and out, sometimes it's poetry, sometimes intelligent doggerel, sometimes quaint. But a great poem. Yes, the poet can use the mind—in fear and trembling. But he must use it.

These comments confirm the studious reader's impression of the fullness and completeness of Frost's poetry; nothing is omitted and, especially in the later poems, Frost's work is wonderfully integrated. Its different elements can hardly be separated without serious dislocation to the total poem.

In the same interview, Frost continues by reflecting usefully on his own views and opinions:

I am not a regionalist. I am a realmist. I write about realms of democracy and realms of the spirit. The land is always in my bones. Someone once asked me if I was for democracy or against it and I could only say that I am so much of it that I didn't know. I have a touchiness about the subject of democracy, of America. It amounts to a touchiness. I know how much difficulty there is about democracy, and how much fun it is too.

When questioned about obscurity in modern verse, Frost replied:

You know, if the obscurity was really a new thought, if it was really that—but if it was a slackness, a not thinking through and getting to the right phrase, I couldn't be bothered with it. The test is when you've worried a poem out. Then you should know whether you've got anything really new—we won't say original, but we can say a fresh thought. For instance, follow what you get out of a man like Matthew Arnold, who was confident and authoritative in his prose and a lost soul in his poetry. You get that lostness in phrase after phrase in his poetry. (It's by phrases that you know a man.) Arnold has explained the academic world to me.

It is easy to see how and why Frost distrusts the academic world; it is not that he abhors knowledge or learning or thought, but rather that he has an absolute dislike and distrust of anything which tampers with the free workings of the human mind and imagination; he wants knowledge, and as much of it as he can acquire. What he does not want, either for himself or for younger writers, is a fixed attitude of mind, the kind of mind which has become fixed because it has settled things finally and coldly by reason alone before it has tested them on the senses, the nerves, and the emotions.

But it must not be concluded that Frost is a believer in flashes of inspiration only. He is convinced that poetry is something given, but he also believes just as firmly that it is something that must be worked for and worked on. The thinker and the craftsman can never be neglected; to ignore them would be, according to Frost, to be unfaithful to his lifelong vocation as a poet.

In *The Paris Review*[7] interview, Frost declared, "I don't want to know too much about myself," meaning perhaps, that he did not wish to probe to the point of mere fruitless introspection. He certainly did not mean that he has never wanted to analyse anything; this becomes very clear when, in the same conversation, he says something about what he believes the nature and origin of poetry to be:

Another thing to say is that every thought, poetical or otherwise, every thought is a feat of association. . . . What do I want to communicate but what a *hell* of a good time I had writing it? The whole thing is performance and prowess and feats of association. Why don't critics talk about those things? . . . One of my ways of looking at a poem right away it's sent to me, right off, is to see if it's rhymed.

Then after expressing horror that any poet should prepare his rhyme-scheme before he begins to write his poem, Frost goes on:

. . . that's very dreadful. It ought to be that you're thinking forward, with the feeling of strength that you're getting them good all the way, carrying out *some intention more felt than thought.* [Italics mine]. It begins. And what is it that guides us—what is it? . . . It's just the same as when you feel a joke coming. . . . And where do these thoughts come from? . . . It's him coming toward you that gives you the animus, you know.

Reading these explanations of the processes which co-operate to produce a poem makes one wish that Frost had himself written more literary criticism. He certainly has all the necessary equipment, together with a unique insight into his own powers. But, of course, if he *had* written much criticism, he would have been a different sort of poet altogether; and he might not have had time to write so many poems of his own.

REFERENCES

1. *P.R.*, p. 89.
2. *Rt. Ft.*, p. 38.
3. *Rt. Ft.*, p. 21.
4. *R.F.*, p. 13.
5. *Rt. Ft.*, p. 18–29.
6. *W.O.*, p. 69.
7. *P.R.*, p. 89.

CHAPTER VI

FROST AND THE CRITICS

Comparatively little criticism has grown up around the formidable body of Frost's work. One or two whole books have been devoted to his poetry and his life, but the most important and useful writings about him tend to be hidden away in magazines and volumes of miscellaneous essays. *Why* Frost has been so neglected is difficult to answer. It may be the traditional air of his work, its use of conventional forms and rhythms, that has prevented the more *avant-garde* critics from showing much interest in his art. Moreover, the fact that Frost was, until his death, a kind of living classic may explain why he is generally accepted but seldom remarked on.

Critics of Frost's work seem to divide themselves roughly into three groups: those who are whole-hearted admirers, those who see dangerous signs both of complacency and unreason in his poetry, and those who admire only certain aspects of his work and are uncertain about the value of the contribution which he has made to modern American poetry.

Like most major poets, Frost has been criticised both for his ideas and for his craftsmanship or lack of it. On the other hand, he himself has suffered—though I doubt if his work has—from too much adulation from uncritical readers who see his poetry as the last great stronghold of tradition and who ignore completely the originality of Frost's mind and the daring accomplishment of his verse. Briefly, he is a poet who appears to cater for every occasion and who seems able to supply whatever mood, emotion, or experience his readers demand of him. This is something which can be said of all significant poets; Frost perhaps suffers from it more than most other important modern poets because his work appears, at a superficial reading, to be so simple and so accessible. Some critics, indeed, even highly intelligent ones, have tended to write about Frost as if it were his fault that his work has been misunderstood in this way.

A. Alvarez[1] is one of those critics who show only a very limited interest in Frost. The reason is that Alvarez is more interested in modernism than in the complete history of modern American poetry; he is, as a result, far more concerned with Pound, Hart Crane and Wallace Stevens, than with such an apparent traditionalist as Frost. He does, however, consider him in the context of the idea of isolation, something which according to Alvarez, American poets are more sensitive to than English poets. Thus he says of Frost:

Perhaps the only modern American poet who really is concerned with manners is Robert Frost, although his are never as complex as those whose absence Trilling laments. Yet I think this is why Frost has been so readily accepted in England; he is peculiarly congenial; we are easy with the tradition of country poetry, simple language and simple wisdom. American cosmopolitanism, even Eliot's, has always appeared a suspicious virtue, whereas Frost seems assured, he does not have to strive; he has New England behind him.

This, as so often with highly sophisticated literary criticism, seems extraordinarily naïve when we are faced with the real complexity of Frost's poems. Like many academic critics, Alvarez has fallen a victim to the fallacy that Frost is a purveyor of home truths, of "simple" wisdom, of barely articulate country opinions. Once we accept these limitations in Alvarez, we can understand why he lays the following charges against Frost's poems:

Frost's insistence on his meaning is to poetry what the
over-use of italics is to prose—more of an irritation than
a help. It gives the impression that he is trying to drum
into an unresponsive audience how moving and profound
the small things of life can be. . . . His generalizations,
instead of coming the hard way, have about them a
touch of simplification, at times almost of glibness. . . .
Granted Frost began to write a very long time ago, so
his archaisms are probably not all deliberate; and
granted his singleness of colloquial tone must have
needed great practice and hard work to perfect.
Nevertheless, the literariness is a surprising contrast
both to his habitual air of plain wisdom and to the
lucidity he reaches in his best work. . . . Frost, too, has
achieved simplicity, but sporadically and as a wit,
rarely in his more direct moral poems. . . . Frost does
at times put more strain on his simplicity than it can
easily bear.

These remarks seem wrong-headed and biassed to the
reader who has studied Frost's poetry carefully. There is,
something almost condescending about Alvarez' attitude
to this fine poet. One is tempted to doubt whether he has
read Frost's total *oeuvre* with the care which it both demands and deserves. For Alvarez' general conclusions
seem to imply that he has only read a few famous
anthology pieces and has failed to consider the compression, precision and profundity of so many of Frost's
poems, particularly those of the middle and later periods.

Louise Bogan[2] is one of those critics who admire Frost's
early work but who have serious doubts about his later
poetry. She says:

Frost's early poems have a simple, unforced lyric
charm; they seem to have been written as naturally
and effortlessly as breathing. . . . Frost is a "countryman". He has a deep love for natural things, for things
of field and pasture, for bird, flower, weed, and tree;

and for the motions and rhythms attendant upon man's
age-old cultivation of the land. . . .

This is the surface Frost, the poet as he appears to those
who know him only from a few anthologies; one is sur-
prised that so sensitive a poet as Louise Bogan should
take such a commonplace and shallow view. However,
she does redeem herself a little when she goes on to say
"In *North of Boston* Frost briefly possessed himself of a
humane realism and insight which he was never quite
able to repeat." Whether one agrees with this or not, one
must admit that it does show a more thoughtful reading
of Frost's poems than we have evidence of in Miss Bogan's
earlier remarks. She rather spoils the value of her criticism, however, when she goes on to describe her dis-
appointment with Frost's later work:

Frost's later work, never completely realized the
tragic power that *North of Boston* promised. In *West-
Running Brook* (1928) he began to play with the role of
self-conscious homespun philosopher. He began to give
reasons for his innate, countryman's conservatism, and
not only reasons, but arguments which were half-
apologies. His own native shrewdness began to get the
upper hand; and, although his lyrical gift remained
very nearly untouched, he began to shift his sympathy,
with almost imperceptible slowness, away from wild-
ness and unpredictability, toward the weather-safe
side of existence. . . .

It is difficult to see what bearing these comments have
upon Frost's later poetry; Miss Bogan appears to have
looked at these poems only very cursorily and it is, surely,
significant that she omits to quote anything on which to
base her judgment. With the exception of *A Masque of
Reason*, there seems to be almost nothing in Frost's more
recent work which could possibly be related to Miss
Bogan's condemnation. However, she is a good deal

H

more sensitive and interesting when she talks of Frost's place in modern American literature than when she generalises about particular groups of his poems:

> His early themes were indeed real, with a reality for which the American expression was starved, and lacking which it would not have achieved, in the following restless years, full balance.... Frost's career has another importance to the America of his time. He restored to a large audience the concept of The Bard— a more acceptable concept than that of The Seer to a society in transition.

This rather two-edged praise does, nevertheless, contain a truth. It is a pity that Miss Bogan has not allowed her undoubtedly penetrating mind to probe more deeply into the complexity and originality of Frost's later work. She herself is satisfied to dismiss this work as a sign that Frost had begun "to slip over, by almost imperceptible degrees, from bitter portrayals of rural facts into a romantic nostalgia for a vanished way of life. . . ." It is odd that Miss Bogan should have missed the stark, and sometimes terrifying, realism of the later poetry.

Cleanth Brooks[3] also has many charges to lay against Frost. His main criticism concerns the subject-matter and general tone of the poetry. Thus he says:

> Frost's anecdotes, incidents, character sketches do have a surface directness; but, as poet, he employs them for purposes of indirection. What sets him off from the poets already discussed is not, for example, a lack of irony, but, first, the context in which the irony appears, and second, the level at which it operates. Characteristically, it appears at the level of licensed whimsy, or of dry understatement. The whimsy is licensed by being made a mannerism of the New England character. That character (it does not concern the present issue whether it is Frost's own character or merely a mask

which he adopts as poet) may be described as follows:
the sensitive New Englander, possessed of a natural
wisdom; dry and laconic when serious; genial and
whimsical when not; a character who is uneasy with
hyperbole and prefers to use understatement to risking
possible overstatement.

Brooks goes on to commend Frost's "solid virtues,"
notably his "strong sense of dramatic decorum," but he is
soon carping again, though with a more telling use of
examples than either Miss Bogan or Alvarez employs.

Much of Frost's poetry hardly rises above the level of
the vignette of rural New England. In general, [his]
metaphors are few and tame; and the occasional bold
metaphor is confined to his very lightest poems. . . .
Frost does not think through his images; he requires
statements. The audacity of his metaphor is thus in
inverse proportion to the seriousness of the experience.

This last remark seems to indicate that Brooks has failed
to examine the fine late poems with much care or detachment. But his most important comments on Frost's
poetry are those which refer to the poet's use of symbols
and to his particular tone:

Frost's themes are frequently stated overtly, outside
the symbolical method; the poet comes downstage to
philosophize explicitly. . . . At his best, of course, Frost
does not philosophize. The anecdote is absorbed into
symbol. The method of indirection operates fully: the
sense of realistic detail, the air of casual comment, are
employed to build up and intensify a serious effect. . . .
In the more ambitious poems Frost's central problem is
to develop depth of feeling without seeming to violate
the realistic and matter-of-fact elements of the situation with which the poem deals.

All this sounds curiously theoretical; while one
admires the happy phrase about anecdote being "absorbed into symbol," one cannot help feeling a little

uneasy about Brooks's hostile remarks. They savour strongly of the study and have that dry, academic quality which Frost himself is always so distrustful of.

Brooks concludes his examination of Frost by asserting that his "best poetry ... exhibits the structure of symbolist metaphysical poetry." This statement seems a fair assessment, as long as the reader does not forget that the tangible realities of Frost's verse also make him, in some sense, a naturalistic poet. For the truth is that he is not the sort of poet to whom the critic can easily attach a label—a fact which may account for the way he has been ignored or treated superficially by so many critics of note. For example, quite a good case could be made out for the assertion that Frost is an impressionistic poet. Labels such as these hint at truths about the poet, but they do not contain the whole truth.

Babette Deutsch,[4] the poet and critic, has made a shrewd and useful analysis of Frost's work. If not markedly original, her comments at least have the virtue of bearing some relation to the poet we know. After remarking that Frost's diction is "simple and colloquial," she continues,

> Frost has about as much to say of happy wooings and matings, of friendly encounters and generous neighbourliness, as of the bleaker aspects of farm life. This, together with the fact that his little dramas are enacted amidst the steady caring for crops and creatures, further distinguishes them from the pomp and circumstance of Robinson's narrative poems, while their humorousness gives them a salty quality not found in Masefield's tales of the English countryside. . . . Frost's poems repeatedly remind us that the central fact in nature for himself and his kind is human nature. . . . However interestedly he may observe such impersonal things as storms and stars, he is apt to relate his observations to some insight into humanity. . . . The grimmer

views that this verse presents are relieved by glimpses of such features of the farmer's day as vivify, if he has the poet's temper, his limited and burdensome routine: the reward of watching the seedling "shouldering its way and shedding the earth crumbs"; the madness of the cow in apple time; the noise of trees. . . .

Miss Deutsch goes on to comment on Frost's apparent remoteness from all the discoveries of the Industrial Revolution. This view is a commonly held one about Frost's work and it would seem to suggest that the poet ignores completely all that urban life implies. This, of course, is nonsense if one remembers the many late poems which are concerned with the discoveries of science. What is certainly true is that Frost prefers country life to city life, though he has always taken the activities and events of an urban civilisation into account.

Miss Deutsch sums up Frost's contribution to modern literature as follows:

There is a Virgilian serenity and solidity about much of this contemporary work [of Frost's], as also a repeated recognition of the tears of things. Where Frost deals with those elements of rural life that have remained unaffected by the rapid technological changes that followed the invention of the steam engine, few poets now writing in English have equalled him, and few of any time or place have surpassed him.

This judgment is far more enthusiastic than either Miss Bogan's or Brooks's. Miss Deutsch seems really to be attempting to get at the truth about Frost, and not to be merely displaying her own cleverness or literary acumen. Her sympathetic summing-up of Frost leads us easily on to the equally laudatory comments of C. Day Lewis.[5] It may be worth noting at this point that the attitudes of English critics show the same variety of opinions as do those of American critics, academic or otherwise. Day

Lewis, of course, writes primarily as a poet who owes a debt to Frost's work. A number of his remarks have already been quoted, but it may be worthwhile making a rapid and compressed selection of some of the others. Thus Day Lewis declares:

If I had to define his poetry in one word, "wise" is the word I should use. Some of his poems have an explicit moral: in others—"The Road Not Taken" or the entrancing "Two Look at Two"—it is a little way beneath the surface: but all his best poems have this hard core of moral truth, a value giving character to their outward features, and growing upon us as we re-read them. . . . [Frost] knows the witless malevolence of Nature. . . . One may say that gossip, and its rich relation, Legend, flourish most heartily where there is a strong sense of community: Robert Frost's narratives, even when they are about solitary people, derive their vigour from that sense: we find in them the countryman's relish for a grim or a humorous tale about his neighbours . . . combined with a subtlety of insight beyond the reach of any crudely instinctive process. . . . Of recent years, Mr. Frost has sought to extend his range yet further, writing a number of poems which directly or indirectly comment upon ideas, upon national affairs and the state of the world, or are at least departures from the subject-matter which he has made his own. The conservatism of the countryman is evident in these poems, and some shrewd blows are delivered. . . . In the more recent books, as in the earlier, the poems I like best are the ones where Robert Frost broods and comments on familiar country things, imperceptibly weaving a pattern, catching a truth in it almost absent-mindedly, like a conjuror reaching down a penny out of thin air. Let us not be deceived by the undemonstrative manner, the apparently casual tone, or fail to recognise a lifetime of devotion behind them

—devotion to his own craft and to the investigating of reality. . . .

This last point is an important one; it shows that there are other ways of meditating on reality than that of Wallace Stevens. Because Frost's is an older and more familiar method, completely divorced from the jargon of modern philosophies, we should be wary of missing the fact that he *is* "investigating reality" in all his best poems. Finally, Day Lewis quotes a remark of Robert Graves's about Frost, a remark with which Day Lewis himself is in very sympathetic agreement. Graves has declared that, of twentieth-century poets, "the best influences for younger writers were Thomas Hardy and Robert Frost." One does not, however, need to be exclusive about this matter of influences; for example, anyone who tried to write poetry nowadays and who had no knowledge of Pound, Eliot, Yeats and Auden, would be in a peculiarly helpless position. Few of us are complete originals. But it is certainly true that Frost can be nothing but a good influence on young poets to-day.

The late F. O. Matthiessen,[6] both in a lecture and in his Introduction to *The Oxford Book of American Verse*, is anxious to place Frost accurately in the history of modern American letters. He says of him:

When the history of American poetry in our time comes to be written, its central figures will probably be Frost and Eliot. They again enforce a whole series of contrasts. Frost does not fit conveniently into either the Whitman tradition or the Poe tradition. The title of his first book, *A Boy's Will*, comes from Longfellow, but his closest ancestor is the more authentic regionalist, Whittier. Twenty-five years old by the turn of the century, Frost still belongs to the older America. He is the poet of the country, of man in nature, as Eliot is the poet of the city, of man in the metropolitan desert.

Frost is also the poet of individualism, in the Emersonian tradition, whereas Eliot, in the darker vein of Hawthorne, has been more aware of the weaknesses of individualism, of the need for the individual to find completion in something larger than himself. . . . They [Eliot and Frost] have in common only what both would consider the leading obligation of the poet: what Frost has called "the renewal of words" and what Eliot has described as an unflagging devotion to the purity of the language, a devotion to its continuity and yet to its continued modification into a more resilient and more capacious instrument for our ever changing needs. . . . Both Frost and Eliot based their metrics on a comparable desire to bring conversational tones into poetry.

This cool, dispassionate criticism is far removed both from the enthusiasm of Day Lewis or Jarrell, and from the anger of Yvor Winters. Matthiessen is content to find a suitable historical context into which to fit Frost. His interest in the poet, in so far as this can be judged from these few comments, is neither passionate nor committed.

In his lecture notes, Matthiessen said very much the same things, though, having more time at his disposal, he went to considerable lengths to demonstrate how little Frost romanticised nature, how much significance he could draw out of simple, natural events, and how adept he was at giving an air of naïveté to poetic forms which were, in fact, highly complex. Matthiessen was eager to show the apparent effortlessness of Frost's work, an effortlessness which concealed years of discipline and a great deal of hidden but conscious artistry.

In his lecture, Matthiessen also pointed out what seemed to him the limitations of Frost's work—his inability to generalise satisfactorily about life, and the lack of depth and intensity in his later poems. On the whole, Matthiessen's remarks about Frost are negative rather than positive; they seem cold and passionless when set beside the two very different kinds of fieriness which we find in Randall Jarrell and Yvor Winters.

Randall Jarrell's essays[7] on Frost have already been quoted extensively. Jarrell always writes as an admirer of the poet's work, but as an admirer who is by no means wholly uncritical. He does, indeed, speak rather harshly of Frost's later work in general, declaring that

> Frost's latest books deserve little more than a foot-note, since they have had few of his virtues, most of his vices, and all of his tricks. . . . *Steeple Bush* has one wonderful poem, "Directive"; a fairly good, dazzlingly heartless one, "The Ingenuities of Debt"; and nothing else that is not done better somewhere else in Frost. . . .

This is altogether too harsh, and it seems a pity that so sensitive and intelligent a critic as Jarrell has aligned himself with those who have little to say for Frost's later poems. Jarrell is undoubtedly right, however, when he says that *A Masque of Mercy* is "a great improvement on the earlier *A Masque of Reason*"; Jarrell finds *A Masque of Reason* "a frivolous, trivial, and bewilderingly corny affair, full of jokes inexplicable except as the contemptuous patter of an old magician certain that *he* can get away with anything in the world"—a view with which one is bound to agree.

If Jarrell is unwilling to admit that Frost's good work is fairly evenly distributed over his early and later books, he has illuminating things to say about the sense of isolation which is such a marked element in the poetry of the older man:

> The older Frost is alone. But it is this loneliness that is responsible for the cold finality of poems like "Neither Out Far Nor In Deep" or "Design".

When he talks of what he thinks is Frost's best work and when he declares that the "best-known poems, with a few exceptions, are not his best poems at all," Jarrell seems to be discovering and honouring the very essence of Frost's great power; discussing the poet's "seriousness" and "honesty," Jarrell says some things which deserve to be quoted in their entirety:

> the bare sorrow with which, sometimes, things are accepted as they are, neither exaggerated nor explained away; the many, many poems in which there are real people with their real speech and real thoughts and real emotions—all this, in conjunction with so much subtlety and exactness, such classical understatement and restraint, makes the reader feel that he is not in a book but in a world, and a world that has in common with his own some of the things that are most important in both. I don't need to praise anything so justly famous as Frost's observation of and empathy with everything in Nature from a hornet to a hillside; *and he has observed his own nature, one person's random or consequential chains of thoughts and feelings, quite as well* [italics mine]. . . . The least crevice of the good poems is saturated with imagination, an imagination that expresses itself in the continual wit and humour and particularity of what is said, in the hard-hewn or hard-polished texture of its saying. The responsibility and seriousness of Frost's best work . . . are nowhere better manifested than in the organisation of these poems: an organisation that, in its concern for any involution or ramification that really belongs to its subject, and in its severity toward anything else, expresses that absorption into a subject that is prior even to affection.

Later, Jarrell goes on to say that Frost's best poetry deserves "the attention, submission, and astonished awe that real art always requires of us."

Briefly, Jarrell makes most of the points that ought to be made about Frost. In my own view, he is too severe with some of the late work, but he makes up for this by the whole-heartedness of his respect and admiration for the poems which he does personally approve of. He holds up for our particular attention "Meeting and Passing," "Design," "Acquainted With the Night," "Directive," "The Subverted Flower," "The Pauper Witch of Grafton," "To Earthward," "The Lovely Shall Be Choosers," "The Fear," "Desert Places," "The Hill Wife," "For Once, Then, Something," "Stopping By Woods on a Snowy Evening," and "Provide, Provide."

Jarrell judges and appraises Frost's best poems not simply as if they were beautiful structures only; he comments on their "use" to us and feels that, like all important art, they not only open up new possibilities to men but also reconcile man to the many inevitable sadnesses and brutalities of life. Frost is, according to Jarrell, not "a brilliant partial poet" but

a complete and representative one. . . . His vision of the world is a complete vision; nothing is concealed or belittled. For this reason, he can always be trusted. Truth, for Frost, is more important than tone of voice, artifice, imagery or music, though he recognises, of course, that these things are the channels through which truth is eased and communicated.

Jarrell has said the most valuable things that I have read about Frost. His criticism is not lengthy but it is pithy, precise and full of wisdom.

Yvor Winters[8] is Frost's most hostile critic. Before we examine in detail his case against the poet, however, it is necessary to give some account of Winters's attitude towards literature and towards poetry in particular. What Winters looks for is, above every other quality, reason; and it is not simply a covert adherence to reason that he demands of all important poets, but a veneration for rationality as a *sine qua non* of all significant poetic statements. His case against Frost thus rests on the belief that the poet is positively anti-reason (a view which it is hard to sustain unless one has read *A Masque of Reason* only).

Winters's critical position with regard to Frost seems to me to be based on two fallacies, one general and the other particular: the first is that poetry is *predominantly* a reasonable (in its literal sense) activity and a method whereby reasonable statements and ideas may be communicated, while the second is that Frost pays *no* attention to reason at all. In the first case, Winters is laying too great a burden on man's rational faculty and too little on his power of intuition (surely the lifespring of poetry?); in the second, he is refusing Frost that measure of reason which is undoubtedly present in his work and which can only be missed by the blinded and thoroughly prejudiced critic. Let us look, then, at some of the charges Winters lays against Frost: "He is a poet of the minor theme, the casual approach and the discreetly eccentric attitude." Since Frost deals boldly with most of the important events and dilemmas of men's lives, it is rather difficult to see what Winters means by this statement, particularly as he does not take the trouble to illustrate his point. But he continues:

I have no objection to the poet's employing rural settings; but we should remember that it is the poet's business to evaluate human experience, and the rural setting is no more valuable for this purpose than any other. . . .

Winters is here, as always, writing as a moralist; he is more concerned with the *good* which poetry does, with poetry as an instrument of instruction and exhortation, than as a unique means of expressing and giving a lasting form to human experience. He does not, however, underrate the importance of artifice or craftsmanship, since he recognises that these things are necessary for any convincing evaluating method.

Winters's main charges against Frost may be summed up in the critic's own words:

> Frost believes in the rightness of impulse, but he does not discuss the pantheistic doctrine which would give authority to impulse. . . . Had Frost been a more intelligent man, he might have seen that the plight of the spiritual drifter was not inevitable, he might have judged it in the light of a more comprehensive wisdom. . . . Frost . . . has wilfully refrained from careful thinking and so is largely responsible for his own condition. . . . Frost, the rustic realist of *North of Boston*, appears in his old age as a standard exemplar of irresponsible Romantic irony, of the kind of irony that has degenerated steadily from the moderately low level of Laforgue, through Pound, Eliot, Cummings and their younger imitators.

"Irresponsible" and "Romantic" seem curiously inept words with which to label the troubled questionings in Frost's later work. As for the general charge of lack of intelligence—it is extraordinarily unjust and wide of the mark.

But Winters's most serious charges against Frost (and it is worth noting the condescension of the critic's attitude, his rather unpleasant air of correcting a disobedient schoolboy) are so wrong-headed that we only need to read almost any handful of Frost's poems to find them triumphantly refuted. Winters says:

> Frost advises us to turn away from serious topics, and for the greater part he confines himself to minor topics. The major topics impinge upon his personal experience, however, for after all they are unavoidable; but his treatment of them is usually whimsical, sentimental, and evasive; and in his latter years his poetry is more and more pervaded by an obscure melancholy which he can neither control nor understand.

Even Winters, however, seems to suspect vaguely that there may be something in Frost which he himself has missed, for he goes on to add, "Yet Frost has a genuine gift for writing, as I have pointed out, and this gift emerges more clearly in his later work than in his earlier, though still hesitantly and momentarily." It is interesting that such a hostile critic should at least have guessed at the significance of Frost's splendid late work. After making this comment, however, Winters proceeds to pick out the few poems of Frost's for which he feels a certain grudging admiration:

> "Acquainted With the Night" . . . seems to me one of the two or three best poems that Frost has written. . . . The understanding of his predicament appears to be greater in this poem than in most of the others; he knows, at least, that it is a predicament and realizes the state of mind to which it has brought him. In the seventh volume, *A Witness Tree*, there is an even more impressive piece entitled "The Most of It". . . . The poem gives one some idea of how great a poet Frost might conceivably have been, had he been willing to use his mind instead of letting it wither.

These remarks seem to spring from something deeper and more obscure than mere misunderstanding and they make one suspect that Winters's enthronement of reason conceals personal prejudices which he himself is unwilling or unable to account for. Certainly, when he criticises Frost's style, as opposed to his content, he makes some very odd remarks; for example, he declares that "although Frost is frequently very skilful in the handling of short rimed forms, he is extremely inept in managing blank verse."

In conclusion, Winters asserts that Frost, though "He is in no sense a great poet, . . . is at times a distinguished and valuable poet," in spite of the fact, it would appear that, according to Winters, Frost's "weakness is commonly, mistaken for wisdom, his vague and sentimental feeling for profound emotion." Winters makes great demands on his poets; indeed, he seems to hold the Romantic view that poets are, or should be, "the unacknowledged legislators of the world." And because he holds this view, he has missed the real importance of Frost—the integrity, affirmation, honest self-questioning, the mind as finely attuned to joy as to suffering and tragedy. But perhaps the very length at which Winters has felt disposed to treat Frost is some indication of how central the poet really is to modern American literature. Frost, in any case, can sustain any number of such attacks. For the truth is that hostile criticism, such as that which Winters proffers, bears little relation to Frost's formidable *oeuvre*. When one reads the poems this sort of criticism seems not only wrong-headed but completely irrelevant. Frost's voice is unmistakably his own, but what he has to say expresses unforgettably our own vague but dark fears in this age of uncertainty.

REFERENCES

1. *S.S.*, p. 169.
2. L. Bogan, *Achievement in American Poetry*, Chicago 1951, p. 47.
3. *M.P.T.*, p. 113.
4. B. Deutsch, *Poetry in Our Time*, New York 1956, p. 61.
5. *R.F.*, p. 13.
6. *O.B.A.V.*, p. xxx.
7. *P.A.*, p. 36.
8. *O.M.P.*, p. 191.

BIBLIOGRAPHY

I. ROBERT FROST

A Boy's Will. London (David Nutt) 1913. New York (Henry Holt) 1915.

North of Boston. London (David Nutt) and New York (Henry Holt) 1914.

Mountain Interval. New York (Henry Holt) 1916.

New Hampshire. New York (Henry Holt) 1923.

West-Running Brook. New York (Henry Holt) 1928.

A Further Range. New York (Henry Holt) 1936.

A Witness Tree. New York (Henry Holt) 1942.

A Masque of Reason. New York (Henry Holt) 1945.

Steeple Bush. New York (Henry Holt) 1947.

A Masque of Mercy. New York (Henry Holt) 1947.

The Complete Poems of Robert Frost. London (Jonathan Cape) 1951.

In the Clearing. New York (Holt, Rinehart and Winston) 1962. [This book was announced after the completion of this study.]

II. OTHERS

ALVAREZ, A.: *The Shaping Spirit*, London 1958.

BROGAN, L.: *Achievment in American Poetry*, Chicago 1951.

BREIT, H. (ed.): *The Writer Observed* (Collier Books) 1961.

BROOKS, C.: *Modern Poetry and the Tradition*, London 1948.

DAY LEWIS, C. (ed.): *Robert Frost. A Selection* (Penguin Books) 1951.

DEUTSCH, B.: *Poetry in Our Time*, New York 1963.

FITZGERALD, R.: *Poetry in Our Time*, New York 1956, in *New Republic*, (8 Aug. 1949).

JARRELL, R.: *Poetry and the Age*, London 1955.

LYNEN, J. F.: *The Pastoral Art of Robert Frost*, New Haven 1960.

MATTHIESSEN, F. O. (ed.): *The Oxford Book of American Verse*, Oxford 1950.

Paris Review (Interview) 1960.

THOMPSON, L.: *Robert Frost*, Minneapolis 1959.

WINTERS, Y.: *On Modern Poets*, New York 1959.